Problem Drinking

ISSUES

Volume 143

Editors

Lisa Firth and Cobi Smith

 **Independence**

Educational Publishers
Cambridge

First published by Independence
PO Box 295
Cambridge CB1 3XP
England

British Library Cataloguing in Publication Data
Problem drinking. - (Issues ; 143)
1. Alcoholism
I. Firth, Lisa II. Smith, Cobi
362.2'92

ISBN-13: 9781861684097

Printed in Great Britain
MWL Print Group Ltd

Cover
The illustration on the front cover is by
Simon Kneebone.

CONTENTS

Chapter One: Alcohol Trends

Chapter Two: Facing Alcohol Abuse

Introduction

Problem Drinking is the one hundred and forty-third volume in the **Issues** series. The aim of this series is to offer up-to-date information about important issues in our world.

Problem Drinking looks at alcohol trends and alcohol abuse.

The information comes from a wide variety of sources and includes:
Government reports and statistics
Newspaper reports and features
Magazine articles and surveys
Website material
Literature from lobby groups
and charitable organisations.

It is hoped that, as you read about the many aspects of the issues explored in this book, you will critically evaluate the information presented. It is important that you decide whether you are being presented with facts or opinions. Does the writer give a biased or an unbiased report? If an opinion is being expressed, do you agree with the writer?

Problem Drinking offers a useful starting-point for those who need convenient access to information about the many issues involved. However, it is only a starting-point. Following each article is an URL to the relevant organisation's website, which you may wish to visit for further information.

* * * * *

Alcohol

Booze, drink, beverage, bev(y), swally

Alcoholic drinks consist mainly of flavoured water and ethyl alcohol (ethanol). They are made by the fermentation of fruits, vegetables or grains. Beer, lager and cider are usually about one part ethanol to 20 parts water although some brands may be twice as strong as others. Wine is about twice to four times as strong and distilled spirits such as whisky, rum and gin are about half water and half ethanol.

Below is some information on the relative strengths of various kinds of alcoholic drinks. The term ABV means 'alcohol by volume' or what percentage of the total liquid is actually alcohol.

The unit of alcohol measure is used to determine medical guidelines as to what are supposed to be safe levels of drinking for men and women per week. Safe drinking limits are given as daily maximums.

Authorities recommend that men should drink no more than three to four units a day and women no more than two to three units a day. It is also suggested that having one or two alcohol free days per week is wise.

What is a unit?:

⇨ One pint of normal strength lager (3 – 3.5%) is equivalent to 2 units

⇨ One 275ml bottle of alcopop (5.5%) is 1.5 units

⇨ a 175ml glass of 12% wine is 2 units

⇨ a single measure of spirits (40%) is 1 unit [1]

These are measures of alcohol as might be bought in a restaurant or pub. Many drinks poured at home will be more generous and so contain more units of alcohol.

Alcopops

Most of these have an ABV of 4 – 5.5% with a range of units from 1.5-1.75 per bottle. The most well-known

brands are the alcoholic lemonades and there are also alcoholic colas, fruit flavoured drinks and those using spirits such as vodka and tequila.

Spirits

Most standard 700 ml bottles of whisky, vodka or rum have an ABV of around 40% containing 25-30 units of alcohol.

Wine

Most wines are produced with an ABV of around 10-13% in a standard 750ml bottle containing 7-10 units of alcohol. Wines from hotter climates such as Italian and Californian wines tend to be stronger at 12 to 13% ABV while those from cooler climates such as Germany are usually 8 to 10%. Therefore a regular pub glass (125ml) of 12% wine is the equivalent of roughly 1.5 units. Fortified wines are even stronger, with drinks like Buckfast and Eldorado being as strong as 17%.

Sherry is usually produced with an ABV of 15-20% giving around 13-14 units of alcohol for a typical 750ml bottle

Cider

This varies in strength from the low alcohol varieties such as Strongbow LA with an ABV of just 0.9% up to the white ciders' with an ABV of around 8.4%. Bottles usually contain 330ml; cans 440ml. A can of one of the stronger ciders contains around 2.5-3.5 units of alcohol.

Beer and lager

Most popular types of bitter beer are around 3.5 to 4.1% ABV – giving around 2 -2.25 units for a pint and 1.5 to 1.75 units for a 440 ml can.

The strength of lager beers can vary widely and ranges from very low strength drinks like Barbican (0.02% ABV) to super strong' lagers at anything up to 10%. But like bitter beers, many popular lagers are around 3.5-4% ABV providing 1.5-1.75 units in a 440ml can and 2-2.25 units in a pint.

A different type of alcohol produced from wood (methyl alcohol) is used in methylated spirits and surgical spirit. Some down and out alcoholics ('meths' drinkers) drink

... HAD ANY ALCOHOL FREE DAYS?

... I'M SAVING THEM UP...

this type of alcohol because it is cheap. Methyl alcohol is poisonous and can cause blindness, coma and death.

Unlike most drugs, alcohol has food value and supplies calories. One gram of alcohol supplies seven calories, almost twice the number of calories as one gram of carbohydrate. A pint of beer can supply as many calories as six slices of bread. Beer provides very little protein or vitamin and distilled spirits provide none at all.

Alcohol is our most popular drug. In England in 2004, 74 per cent of men and 59 per cent of women reported drinking an alcoholic drink on at least one day in the week prior to interview. Fifteen per cent of men and 8 per cent of women reported drinking on every day in the previous week. Thirty-nine per cent of men and 22 per cent of women had drunk more than the recommended number of units on at least one day in the week prior to interview.

Older people were more likely to drink regularly – 30 per cent of men and 19 per cent of women aged 45-64 drank on five or more days in the week prior to interview compared to 8 per cent of men and 5 per cent of women aged 16-24. Younger people were more likely to drink heavily, with 48 per cent of men and 39 per cent of women aged 16-24 drinking above the daily recommendations compared to 19 per cent of men and 5 per cent of women aged 65 and over

In the UK in 2004, 61 per cent of people reported that they had heard of the government guidelines on alcohol intake. [2]

Young people drink more alcohol than older people. In the late teens and early twenties alcohol consumption is 40-50% higher. Despite the licensing laws about 60 per cent of 13 -17 year olds have bought alcohol in a pub or off-licence. The proportion of 11-15-year-olds who drink alcohol at least once a week has risen from 20% in 1988 to 24% in 2000 [3]. Some of this is in the home drinking small amounts. However, many young people also drink in pubs and clubs as well as on the streets or in parks.

Young people tend to get drunk more often, drink more in one session and drink stronger beers, lagers and ciders. The last few years have seen new drinks coming on to the market which are targeted at the younger age group. Extra strong lagers and ciders have been followed by alcopops' – drinks with high alcoholic strength which do not taste of alcohol.

The UK has over 80,000 pubs and similar 'on-licensed' premises, over 50,000 off-licenses (an increasing

Alcohol is our most popular drug

number of which are in super-markets), plus over 60,000 licensed restaurants and clubs.

Restrictions on advertising alcohol are less stringent than with tobacco. Unlike tobacco, alcohol is regularly advertised on T.V. Adverts are not supposed to be directed at young people, encourage excessive use or to link drink with driving.

The law

The manufacture, sale, distribution and purchase of alcohol is mainly controlled by the 1964 Licensing Act.

There are different licences governing the sale of alcohol. Full 'on licenses' are granted to pubs and clubs and mean alcohol can be drunk on the premises. 'Off licenses' are granted to off-licenses, shops and supermarkets where alcohol cannot be consumed on the premises. 'Restaurant licenses' permit the sale of alcohol and consumption on the premises if accompanied by a meal. Licensing laws also restrict the times at which alcohol can be sold and consumed.

There are also rather complex laws about the age at which people can drink alcohol:
⇨ It is an offence to give alcohol to a child under 5 years old.
⇨ Children of any age can go into parts of pubs that are set aside for meals or as family rooms.
⇨ Children aged over 14 years can go into pubs unaccompanied by adults but cannot be served alcohol until they are 18 years old.
⇨ Young people are not allowed to drink alcohol in a bar or buy alcohol in a pub or off licence until they are 18 years old.
⇨ 16 year olds can buy and drink beer or cider (but not spirits) in a pub but only if they are having a meal.
⇨ There are slightly different rules in different parts of the UK In Northern Ireland, for example, nobody can enter any part of a pub if they are under 18 years old.

Anyone aged under 18 years old who tries to buy alcohol can be fined but this rarely happens. A licensed vendor (pub landlord, off licence proprietor etc.) who knowingly sells alcohol to young people aged under 18 years can be fined and could lose their licence. Licenses have to be approved by magistrates and the police can object if they think vendors are not fit to sell alcohol.

Unlicensed 'home brewing' of beers, ciders and wines (but not spirits) is permitted but it is illegal to sell these products.

Under the Public Order Act 1986, it is an offence to possess or carry alcohol on trains, coaches or minibuses travelling to or from certain sporting events. Police also have powers to confiscate alcohol from under 18s, if they are drinking on the streets. Some cities, such as

Bath and Coventry, have introduced by-laws making it an offence to drink alcohol on the streets in city centre areas at any age.

It is an offence to be drunk and disorderly in a public place, including within licensed premises. It is also an offence to drive whilst unfit to do so because of drink. Anything more than 80mg of alcohol in every 100ml of blood is over the legal limit. This usually works out at about two and a half pints of normal strength beer for males but varies from person to person and is usually less for females.

Effects/risks

Alcohol is absorbed into the bloodstream and starts to have an effect within 5 to 10 minutes. The effect can last for several hours, depending on the amount consumed. The effect will also depend on:

⇨ how quickly it is drunk, whether there is food in the stomach and the person's body weight.

⇨ how used to drinking someone is, in other words, what their tolerance is to alcohol.

⇨ how people feel before they are drinking. People who feel relaxed and in a good mood are less likely to become aggressive. Some people 'drown their sorrows' in drink and find they feel worse than ever after.

After about two pints of beer most people feel less inhibited and more relaxed. Alcohol is a depressant drug. It acts on the central nervous system to slow the body down. Some people become aggressive and argumentative, especially men. A lot of violence on the streets and in the home (much of it directed at women and children) happens after people have been drinking.

After about 4 pints of average strength beer, drinkers become uncoordinated and slur their speech.

Drinking alcohol makes accidents more common, especially when people fall over, drive or are operating machinery. Lowering of inhibitions can make it more likely that people will put themselves in sexual situations which they later regret. They are also less likely to practice safer sex and use condoms if they have intercourse. Drinking too much in one go can lead to losing consciousness and death by choking on vomit.

Alcohol can also be very dangerous to take in combination with other drugs, especially other depressant drugs such as barbiturates, heroin, methadone or tranquillisers and drugs such as anti-depressants, anti-histamines and painkillers. Mixing these drugs and alcohol has led to many fatal overdoses.

Long term, heavy drinking can be very damaging. Physical dependence and tolerance develop so people drink more and more and suffer withdrawal symptoms (such as trembling, sweating, anxiety and delirium) if they try to stop. At this point people will be regarded as alcoholics. Heavy, long term drinking can also lead to damage to the heart, liver, stomach and brain and lead to obesity.

' I was dry for almost a month but at my cousin's wedding I felt different from the others. I decided to have one drink. I thought I could control it ...... I drank without restraint for the next five days. In a blinding flash of drunken logic I saw how bad I was. It was a shattering thunderbolt. I took a handful of pills, not as a cry for help but because of the hopeless position I was in.' N. Kessel and H. Walton Alcoholism Penguin 1965.

Pregnant women who drink six of more units of alcohol a day may give birth to babies who suffer withdrawal symptoms and also have facial abnormalities and possible retarded physical and mental development which together is called foetal alcohol syndrome. However such cases are rare in the UK. Lesser degrees of drinking during pregnancy may result in a baby being born with a low birth weight but there is little evidence that moderate drinking during pregnancy causes harm to the mother or her baby. See the Foetal Alcohol Syndrome Aware UK site for much more on this

Excessive drinking commonly aggravates personal, family, work and financial problems and contributes towards family breakdown, violence and other forms of crime associated with loss of control.

The number of alcohol related deaths (where alcohol is mentioned on the death certificate) have increased almost every year since 1979. Numbers of deaths more than doubled in this period from 2,506 in 1979 to 5,543 in 2000 [5]

A higher figure of 22,000 people is the estimate for the number of deaths where alcohol is a contributory factor (eg in accidents).[6]

Men should drink no more than three to four units a day and women no more than two to three units a day

Alcopops are alcoholic drinks which do not taste of alcohol such as alcoholic lemonades and fruit juices. Some people say they have been deliberately made by companies who make alcohol to get the younger age range to start drinking and to get them to drink more. Younger children often do not like the taste of alcohol when they first try it. Alcopops do not have the taste. Drinking alcopops can also make it easier to get drunk without realising it. Many alcopops have a high alcohol content.

See also Drug interactions and the website of Alcohol Concern for the latest news and reports on alcohol use in the UK.

References
[1] Source: Factsheet 8. Health Impacts of Alcohol. Alcohol Concern, Winter 2002/2003.
[2] Source: UK. The Information Centre: Statistical Bulleting. Statistics on Alcohol: England, 2006.
[3] Source: Young People and Alcohol. Wired for Health, 2003.
[4] Source: The Revenue Effect of Changing Alcohol Duties. IFS, 1999.
[5] Source: Health Statistics Quarterly, 17. HMSO, Spring 2003.
[6] Source: Interim Analytical Report. Strategy Unit Alcohl Harm Reduction Project, 2004.
Updated October 2006

⇨ The above information is reprinted with kind permission from DrugScope. Visit www.drugscope.org.uk for more information.

Alcohol myths and facts

Information from Alcohol Focus Scotland

promoting responsibility,
reducing harm, changing culture

Black Coffee will sober me up

Only TIME can sober you up. The idea that drinking coffee will sober you up is a complete myth. In fact, the stimulant effect of caffeine actually increases the rate at which any drug is absorbed, so any alcohol in the stomach will reach the bloodstream even faster than it otherwise would. Being sick or having a cold shower are also myths – these things can do nothing to affect the alcohol already in your body. Only the passage of time will affect the 'sobering up' process. The liver can process approximately one unit of alcohol each hour. It starts processing alcohol 20 minutes after the first drink has been taken.

Alcohol is a stimulant

Alcohol is a depressant. This surprises many people who think that alcohol must be a stimulant because it seems to increase sociability. The reason for this is that alcohol first depresses the part of the brain which controls our behaviour and our inhibitions. Alcohol seems to be stimulating us when in fact we are simply becoming less inhibited.

Alcohol will warm you up

Alcohol actually increases heat loss from the body. The 'warm glow' that you feel is the heat leaving your body through the skin as the peripheral circulation is increased. Giving anyone alcohol to warm them up is a very dangerous thing to do and would actually increase the risk of hypothermia in an elderly person.

The limit for drink driving in the UK is 80mg%

The legal limit for drinking and driving in the UK is 80mg of alcohol per 100ml of blood (BAC), or 35 microgrammes per 100ml of breath (Br AC) People often ask what does this mean in terms of the number of drinks they can safely have. In actual fact, it is different for every person as various factors need to be taken into account. For example a person's body weight, gender, the strength of the drink etc. In terms of safety, the answer would be none – one drink will affect your judgement and reaction time. 80mg% is actually higher than most other Europeans countries where the limit is 50mg%.

The idea that drinking coffee will sober you up is a complete myth

---

Binge drinking won't harm you if you are young

Although binge drinking when you are young doesn't necessarily mean that you will develop a drink problem, or become alcohol dependent there are plenty other ways it can harm you. You are much more likely to have an accident or harm yourself when you have been drinking too much. Accident and emergency wards are full of people who have harmed themselves in some way during a big drinking session. Remember too, that heavy drinking when you are young can lead to long term health problems

You can drink as much red wine as you like because it is good for your health

Any health benefits derived from drinking red wine only apply to men over 45 and post menopausal women. And these benefits are not exclusive to red wine – the same can be got from a low salt and high fruit and vegetable diet.

It is illegal for bar staff to serve people who are already drunk

Although it is illegal to serve a drunk person very often this law is completely overlooked.

Alcohol begins to affect the brain within 5 minutes of being swallowed

Yes, it's that quick. Alcohol begins to affect the brain in 5 minutes and the liver begins to absorb alcohol around 20 minutes after the first drink has been taken.

'Hair of the dog' is the best cure for a hangover.

The best cure for a hangover is simply time and plenty of water to re-hydrate the system.

⇨ The above information is re-printed with kind permission from Alcohol Focus Scotland. For more information on this and other alcohol-related issues, please visit their website at www.alcohol-focus-scotland.org.uk

© Alcohol Focus Scotland

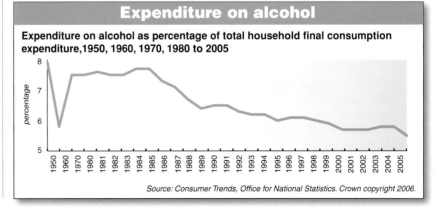

Expenditure on alcohol

Expenditure on alcohol as percentage of total household final consumption expenditure,1950, 1960, 1970, 1980 to 2005

Source: Consumer Trends, Office for National Statistics. Crown copyright 2006.

Cutting teen drinking

Alcohol at home can cut teenage binge drinking, study says

By Polly Curtis, health correspondent

Teenagers who drink alcohol with their parents are less likely to binge drink, according to a survey of 10,000 children which backs the continental style of introducing teenagers to small amounts of alcohol early.

Parents who do not want their children drinking behind their backs should limit their pocket money to less than £10 a week, says the study, carried out by academics and trading standards officers.

> **Girls from the most socially deprived areas who received the most weekly pocket money were the most likely to drink irresponsibly**

It found that teenagers who illegally bought their own alcohol were six times as likely to drink in public, in parks and on the streets, three times as likely to be regular drinkers and twice as likely to be binge drinkers.

Mark Bellis, the lead researcher and director of the public health centre at Liverpool John Moores University, said: "We are too used to handing £10 or £20 to young people without any realisation of where it is being spent. Add to that birthday money and money from part-time jobs – young people have money to spend. Parents need to know more about what their children are spending it on."

The report calls on the government to force the alcohol industry to stop marketing to teenagers and to crack down on shops selling to underage teenagers. Some 40% of the 15- and 16-year-olds polled who reported that they drank said they bought their own alcohol.

The survey was carried out in more than 130 schools in the north-west of England by trading standards officers. More than 10,000 questionnaires were returned by pupils aged 15 and 16. The results suggest that girls from the most socially deprived areas who received the most weekly pocket money were the most likely to drink irresponsibly – defined as more than twice a week, five units at a time and in public spaces.

Nearly 90% drank at least once every six months. Some 40% of those binged regularly, a quarter drank frequently and half drank in public. Those who were most at risk, who did all three, were most likely to buy the alcohol themselves or through an older sibling or friend. People who drank with their parents, and received less than £10 pocket money a week, exhibited the safest behaviour.

Other research has shown that the worst problems associated with teenage drinking happen when it takes place in public, in contrast with France and Italy, where young people typically first drink at mealtimes with their parents.

Today's findings contrast sharply with a recent call from Alcohol Concern to prosecute parents who give their under-15s alcohol. Professor Bellis said that this evidence showed that approach was flawed. "I don't think prosecuting parents is the way forward. It's possibly the worst thing you can do to a child at that stage."

A spokesman for Alcohol Concern said: "The drinks industry has a major role to play in cutting down alcohol purchasing by underaged drinkers."

A Department of Health spokesperson said alcohol sales to under-18s were decreasing. "We are working closely with the industry to encourage the responsible sale of alcohol. In 2005, restrictions on alcohol advertising on TV were tightened."

11 May 2007

Alcohol use internationally

Information from the World Health Organization

Although alcohol consumption has occurred for thousands of years, many of the varied health effects have been discovered fairly recently. Alcohol consumption has health and social consequences via intoxication (drunkenness), dependence (habitual, compulsive and long-term drinking), and other biochemical effects. In addition to chronic diseases that may affect drinkers after many years of heavy use, alcohol contributes to traumatic outcomes that kill or disable at a relatively young age, resulting in the loss of many years of life to death or disability. There is increasing evidence that besides volume of alcohol, the pattern of the drinking is relevant for the health outcomes. Overall there is a causal relationship between alcohol consumption and more than 60 types of disease and injury. Alcohol is estimated to cause about 20-30% worldwide of oesophageal cancer, liver cancer, cirrhosis of the liver, homicide, epilepsy, and motor vehicle accidents.

> **Alcohol is estimated to cause about 20-30% worldwide of oesophageal cancer, liver cancer, cirrhosis of the liver, homicide, epilepsy, and motor vehicle accidents**

Worldwide alcohol causes 1.8 million deaths (3.2% of total) and 58.3 million (4% of total) of Disability-Adjusted Life Years (DALYs). Unintentional injuries alone account for about one third of the 1.8 million deaths, while neuro-psychiatric conditions account for close to 40% of the 58.3 million DALYs. The burden is not equally distributed among the countries, as is shown on the map below.

Globally alcohol consumption has increased in recent decades, with all or most of that increase in developing countries. This increase is often occurring in countries with little tradition of alcohol use on population level and few methods of prevention, control or treatment. The rise in alcohol consumption in developing countries provides ample cause for concern over the possible advent of a matching rise in alcohol-related problems in those regions of the world most at risk.

⇨ The above information is reprinted with kind permission from the World Health Organization. Visit www.who.int for more information.

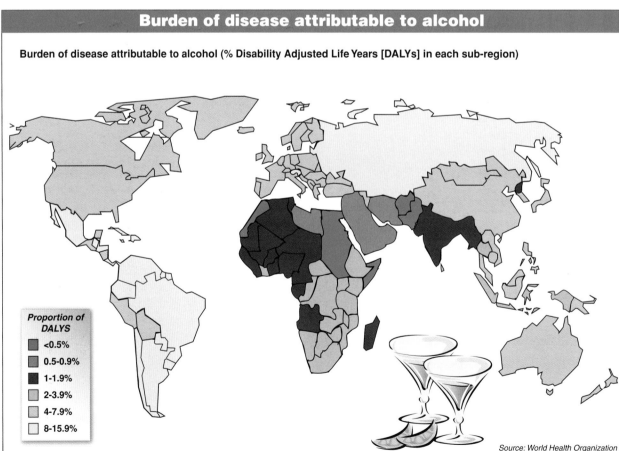

Burden of disease attributable to alcohol

Burden of disease attributable to alcohol (% Disability Adjusted Life Years [DALYs] in each sub-region)

Proportion of DALYS
- <0.5%
- 0.5-0.9%
- 1-1.9%
- 2-3.9%
- 4-7.9%
- 8-15.9%

Source: World Health Organization

Factors affecting drink

Alcohol affects everyone differently. Here's what influences the effects of booze on you

Your gender: The average adult male is made up of 66% fluid, compared to 55% for women. This means any alcohol intake winds up more diluted in the bloke's body. As a result, women are more likely to get drunk faster than men on the same booze intake.

Your age: Sensible drinking guidelines are aimed at people aged 18 and above. This is because we all mature at different rates, which includes your liver development – crucial in the processing of alcohol in the body.

Your physical shape: Your size, weight and height influence the effect of alcohol on your body. The bigger you are, the more blood you have in your body. This means that as you drink, the alcohol concentration in your bloodstream will rise at a slower rate than your short-ass boozing buddy.

Your relationship with drink: Drink on a regular basis and your mind and body can become tolerant to alcohol. This means it gets used to the presence of booze and encourages you to drink more to feel the same effect. So if you're drinking with someone who's never had a pint before, chances are they'll hit the floor before you can say: 'same again, then?'

The type of drink: The effects of some alcoholic drinks work faster than others. For example, the body absorbs fizzy drinks such as alcopops, champagne or cider, more rapidly than stuff like wine or whiskey. Also consider the percentage alcohol per volume of your chosen tipple. The greater the percentage, the less you need to feel the effects.

The rate you drink: The faster you drink, the quicker the effects kick in, but it may also take you by surprise. So pace yourself, people.

When you last ate: Alcohol is absorbed into the bloodstream via the stomach. So if you haven't eaten, the drink could go straight to your

head. If you know you're going to be drinking, eat a decent meal first to help slow down the absorption rate.

Your mood: Alcohol is a depressant drug, so if you're down when you're drinking then chances are you'll wind up feeling worse.

Who you're with: The effects of drinking alcohol are more likely to be apparent if you're mixing with people at the time. This is because we tend to be more outwardly expressive around others.

Where you're at: If you're sitting in the pub with mates, then chances are you're going to be supping on something. Had you met at the gym, this wouldn't be happening.

⇨ The above information is reprinted with kind permission from TheSite.org. Visit their website at www.thesite.org for more information.

© TheSite.org

Clever girls are more likely to binge-drink

Young women are more likely to binge-drink if they are well educated, says a study.

But the reverse is true in later life as those with fewer qualifications start drinking more heavily in their 40s.

Researchers believe the difference could be down to the fact that better-educated females tend to put off child rearing while less-educated ones have children earlier and are more likely to drink heavily when the children are grown up.

The type of jobs linked to higher and lower qualifications also contributes to contrasting drinking habits, the study found.

It examined the habits of 11,500 British men and women born during one week in March 1958. They were monitored and surveyed about how much and how often they drank at the ages of 23, 33 and 42.

Binge-drinking was classed as having ten or more units of alcohol – a half pint of lager, small glass of wine or pub measure of spirits – on one occasion for men and seven or more for women.

Less-educated men were found to be around three times more likely to be binge-drinkers at all times of their life than well-educated men.

Highly-educated women, however, were about one third more likely to binge drink at 23 than those with no or few qualifications.

By 42, women with no or few qualifications were more than twice as likely as their highly qualified peers to be binge-drinking.

Barbara Jefferis of the Institute of Child Health, who wrote the report of the study – published today in the Journal of Epidemiology and Community Health – said more research was needed to explain the differences between the two sets of women.

⇨ This article first appeared in the *Daily Mail*, 17 January 2007

© Associated Newspapers Ltd 2007

Drinking

Fewer men exceeding benchmarks

The proportion of men in Great Britain exceeding the government's daily sensible drinking benchmarks fell from 39 per cent in 2004 to 35 per cent in 2005. Women are less likely than men to exceed the benchmarks, with 20 per cent of women exceeding the sensible drinking benchmark on at least one day in the previous week in 2005.

In 2005, 72 per cent of men and 57 per cent of women had had an alcoholic drink on at least one day during the previous week

In 2005, 72 per cent of men and 57 per cent of women had had an alcoholic drink on at least one day during the previous week.

Government guidelines on sensible drinking are based on daily benchmarks of between three and four units per day for men and two to three units per day for women. In 2006, knowledge of daily benchmarks and measuring alcohol in units had increased among both men and women. The proportion of adults

who had heard of daily benchmarks increased from 54 per cent in 1997 to 69 per cent.

Younger people were more likely than older people to exceed the daily benchmarks. Over two fifths (42 per cent) of young men aged 16 to 24 had exceeded four units on at least one day during the previous week. This compares with 16 per cent of men aged 65 and over. Among women, 36 per cent of those in the youngest age group had exceeded three units on at least one day compared with only 4 per cent of those aged 65 and over.

Heavy drinking – defined as over eight units a day for men and six units a day for women on at least one day during the previous week – was more common among men (19 per cent) than women (8 per cent).

Heavy drinking was also more common among young people: 31 per cent of men and 22 per cent of women aged 16 to 24 had drunk

heavily on at least one day during the previous week. Among those aged 65 and over, these proportions were just 4 per cent and 1 per cent respectively.

The recent upward trend in heavy drinking among young women may have peaked. The proportion of 16 to 24 year old women who had drunk more than six units on at least one day in the previous week increased from 24 per cent to 28 per cent between 1998 and 2002 but has since fallen to 22 per cent in 2005.

Source

General Household Survey, 2005; National Statistics Omnibus Survey 2006

Notes

Obtaining reliable information about drinking behaviour is difficult. Surveys consistently record lower levels of consumption than would be expected from data on alcohol sales. This is partly because people may under-estimate how much alcohol they consume.

Surveys derive alcohol consumption estimates from assumptions about the alcohol content of drinks, combined with information about the volume drunk. Over the last twenty years new types of alcoholic drink have been introduced, alcohol content of some drinks has increased and they are now sold in more variable quantities. Different surveys try to keep pace with these changes but quite often they develop independently. They may use different assumptions in estimating alcohol consumption and this may affect the comparability of results between surveys.

Published on 28 November 2006

⇨ The above information is reprinted with kind permission from the Office for National Statistics. Visit www.statistics.gov.uk for more information.

The mid-life bingers

If you thought only the young drank to excess, think again. That oh-so-civilised half bottle a night may be more than your ageing body can cope with . . .

The ladette slumped in the gutter, the lad throwing up in the street – these are the familiar images of the 'binge' drinker. But what about the fifty-something couple sharing a bottle of claret with supper every night? It will come as a surprise to many, but according to a new report they, too, are drinking to excess.

SO...
ONE GLASS
THREE TIMES A DAY?
...OR THREE GLASSES
ONCE A DAY?
...OR AM I
GETTING CONFUSED
WITH MY
MEDICATION?

'Society is fixated on the alcohol problems caused by young people who binge drink in public, or the small number of alcoholics who are literally drinking themselves to death,' says Andrew McNeil, director of the Institute of Alcohol Studies.

'We should be far more worried about the tens of thousands of middle-aged people who risk liver and brain damage through a drip-drip effect of persistent alcohol consumption.'

'It's their health problems and their health bills that are going to really give the country a headache over the next two or three decades,' he says.

'It does not matter whether people are paying a fortune for fine wines or knocking back plonk – it's the amount of alcohol consumed that does the damage.'

The baby boomer generation – born between 1945 and 1965 – grew up with unprecedented access to alcohol.

Many of those who stick to the recommended two or three drinks a day make that their daily minimum, rather than a maximum level that is only infrequently consumed

---

As social mores changed, so did attitudes to alcohol – wine particularly had previously been regarded as a 'treat,' but increasingly became an essential part of people's social lives.

As a result, the baby boomers are on course for serious chronic, alcohol-related illness over the next two or three decades, experts warn.

This middle-aged health hazard has gone unnoticed until now because of the widespread assumption that people cut down on drinking as they grew older and wiser.

But a new report, Alcohol and Ageing, published by NHS Health Scotland, says this has not happened with the baby boomers.

'It's now becoming clear that the generation before the baby boomers have always drunk less than those born post-war – and have taken this into old age,' says Dr Laurence Gruer, director of the Public Health Science Directorate in Scotland.

'This baby-boomer generation, however, appears to have little intention of becoming more abstemious with age.'

Compared with today's pensioners, twice as many 45 to 65-year-olds regularly consume more than the recommended safe levels of drinking.

And many of those who stick to the recommended two or three drinks a day make that their daily minimum, rather than a maximum level that is only infrequently consumed.

According to Professor Mary Gilhooly, head of gerontology research at Glasgow Caledonian University, the problem with current sensible drinking limits is that people see them as applying to all age groups.

'Yet the body's ability to metabolise alcohol decreases with age – so that sensible drinking limits for 25 to 30-year-olds are not sensible as you get older.'

'There is certainly evidence that moderate alcohol consumption, particularly of red wine, protects against heart attacks and strokes and is associated with healthy ageing,' she says.

'However, the term 'moderate' refers to much lower levels of alcohol than most baby boomers imagine – certainly lower than the upper limit of recommended sensible drinking levels.'

And once you go above light-to-moderate consumption, then the older you are the more harm that alcohol does to your body.

'Older people's liver and kidneys function less efficiently, so they have higher blood-alcohol levels for longer than younger people who have drunk the same amount,' explains Professor Gilhooly.

In the short-term, this means longer and more intense hangovers.

In the longer term, regular drinking will damage the brain, the liver, the pancreas and the nervous system, causing depression, anxiety, diabetes, obesity and liver disease.

A further concern is that from their 40s onwards, many people are already loading their livers with regular medication for high blood pressure, diabetes or other chronic illnesses.

'Any oral medication is going to be making the liver work harder,' says Bob Batten, research co-ordinator at the National Addiction Centre, at King's College London.

> 'We need to get the message across that alcohol damage can occur to people of all classes and education, including those who feel in control of their drinking'

'There's also growing evidence that alcohol exacerbates many unpleasant side-effects of prescription medication.'

'Alcohol consumption can increase the effects of anti-hypertensive medication, as well as the sedative effect of analgesics and anti-depressants.'

'Accident and emergency doctors frequently see older people who are on regular medication and who have fallen and broken an arm or leg because they have become confused or lost their sense of balance after a couple of drinks,' he said.

Experts also warn that regular 'safe' drinking in early middle age may become problem drinking later on, as a response to stresses of old age such as retirement, ill-health and bereavement.

'It's a real concern that relatively high alcohol consumption is seen as normal, acceptable and even medicinal by so many people approaching a major lifestyle change such as retirement,' says Dr Gruer.

'The fear is that people who grew up in the 1960s tend to think they can get away with a party lifestyle indefinitely.'

'Yet people like Mick Jagger and other Sixties' icons who have kept their careers alive well into the 21st century are normally fitness fanatics who barely touch alcohol.'

So far, there is no consensus on what is the 'safe' amount of alcohol for the over 45s.

Alcohol Concern's leaflet on safer drinking for over-60s, I Don't Mind If I Do, simply states that current recommendations (2-3 units daily for women and 3-4 units for men) 'might be too much for some older people', especially if they are on medication or have particular health problems.

'The research simply isn't available,' says Professor Gilhooly, 'to allow us to make definite recommendations as to how much alcohol is safe for 45 to 65-year-olds.'

Levels will, in any case, always vary slightly between individuals.

Yet it is very clear that in order to remain healthy in old age, the baby-boomer generation should ensure that they drink at very modest levels.

In America, the U.S. National Institute on Alcohol Abuse and Alcoholism sets limits for the over 65s of one drink a day – and the suggestion is that the 45 to 65s start trying to wean themselves to this stage before it's too late.

Dr Gruer believes that an awareness of the need to reduce alcohol consumption with age should be part of every pre-retirement programme.

Alcohol Concern's advice to the over-60s includes practical suggestions to help pensioners lose the alcohol habit: drinking slowly with food, having alcohol-free days and meeting friends in cafes or clubs rather than pubs.

'We need to get the message across that alcohol damage can occur to people of all classes and education, including those who feel in control of their drinking,' says Dr Jeff French of the Social Marketing Centre.

'The social norm for older people should be one very pleasant glass of wine, probably with dinner. If you are going to drive, don't drink at all. Such changes can make a big difference to your health.'

As 61-year-old Kay Brayford, who runs a B&B in Oxfordshire, recently discovered.

'I've always drunk in moderation – but the older I got, the more I was finding I couldn't cope with a couple of glasses of wine in the evening.'

'I'd have an absolute blank the next day and couldn't remember what I'd done. I became increasingly depressed, too. Friends the same age were complaining of the same thing.'

'My GP suggested I cut back, and the most I drink now is a glass of wine a day. I've noticed a real difference. I feel more motivated and am able to keep busy. I hadn't realised that alcohol could affect older people in this way.'

⇨ This article first appeared in the Daily Mail, 26 September 2006

© 2007 Associated Newspapers Ltd

Watch out, it's stronger than you realise

Health guidelines set out a maximum weekly alcohol intake of 14 units for women and 21 for men. However, the belief that one glass of wine equals one unit is only true when that glass contains 125ml and the wine is around 8 per cent ABV (alcohol by volume).

Today, many wines are 12 or 13 per cent ABV, and most standard wine glasses contain 175ml – 2.3 units – and larger wine glasses contain 250ml, which is equal to 3 units. 'A decade ago, we used to like small, crystal glasses – but now most customers choose a large, plain wine glass,' said a spokesman for John Lewis, whose best-selling wine glass, the Vino Large, holds 500ml.

And as with wine, the strength of beer and lager has also increased – and a pint of stronger beer is now the equivalent of three units.

According to the US National Institute on Alcohol Abuse and Alcoholism, a safe daily limit for those aged 65 and over is just one unit of alcohol a day. That means half a pint of normal-strength beer, one measure of spirits, a 50ml glass of sherry or a 125ml glass of wine.

According to the UK Medical Council on Alcoholism, the definition of 'light drinking' is fewer than eight units a week for men and fewer than six for women.

Drinking: adults' behaviour and knowledge in 2006

Summary

Knowledge of units and benchmarks

Eighty six per cent of people said that they had heard of measuring alcohol consumption in units – an increase from 83 per cent in 2004.

Fifty eight per cent of those who had drunk beer in the last year knew that a unit of beer is half a pint but one in five (20 per cent) gave an amount that was wrong.

Knowledge of units among both men and women had increased between 1998 and 2006: for example, the proportion of men who drank beer who knew that a unit of beer is half a pint increased from 49 per cent in 1997 to 61 per cent in 2006. Similarly, the proportion of women who drank wine who knew that a unit of wine is a glass increased from 51 per cent in 1998 to 68 per cent in 2006.

Drinkers who had heard of units were asked whether or not they kept a check on the number of units they drank: 13 per cent said that they did (similar to the 2002 figure of 11 per cent and the 2004 figure of 13 per cent).

There has been an increase from 54 per cent in 1997 to 69 per cent in 2006 in the proportion of the sample who had heard of daily benchmarks.

Having heard of daily recommended levels did not necessarily mean that people knew what they were – 15 per cent (wrongly) thought that the recommended daily maximum for men was five units or more, and 10 per cent thought that for women, it was four units or more. There was no significant change in the knowledge of benchmark levels over the survey years.

Discussion of drinking with GPs or other health professionals

About one male drinker in seven (14 per cent) had discussed drinking in the last year with their GP or someone else at the surgery, or a doctor or other medical person elsewhere. This was higher than in 2004, when 11 per cent of male drinkers had discussed drinking with a medical person. Women were less likely to have had discussions (only eight per cent had done so). There was no significant change since 2000 among women.

Places where people buy alcohol

The outlets where people were most likely to have bought alcohol in the last year were supermarkets (70 per cent), licensed bars (66 per cent), and restaurants (62 per cent).

The percentage of respondents who had bought alcohol from an off-licence or from a licensed bar in the past year fell over the survey period. Purchases from a restaurant increased from 57 per cent to 62 per cent over the same time period. The percentages for purchases from a branch of a supermarket or from other retail outlets were very similar to those found in previous survey years.

Men were twice as likely as women to have bought alcohol from a bar in the past week either for themselves or others to drink (36 per cent compared with 18 per cent) and twice as likely to have bought alcohol from an off-licence (8 per cent compared with four per cent).

There was no difference overall in the proportions of men and women who had bought alcohol at a supermarket in the previous week: 24 per cent of both men and women had done so.

There was very little change over time in the percentages of people who had bought alcohol from different outlets in the previous week, with the exception of licensed bars where the percentage of people who had bought alcohol in the past week fell from 29 per cent in 2004 to 26 per cent in 2006.

Awareness of unit labelling

Nearly a third (32 per cent) of drinkers who had heard of units had seen unit labelling on alcohol, a significant increase from 23 per cent in 2000 but no change since 2004.

The most frequently mentioned outlet where unit labelling had been seen was a supermarket or shop (86 per cent). Pubs were mentioned by 22 per cent, off licences by 21 per cent, six per cent mentioned restaurants and four per cent nightclubs.

What people drink

Half of all alcohol drunk was beer – 42 per cent was normal strength beer and a further 10 per cent was strong beer (defined as being six per cent or more alcohol by volume). Over a quarter (28 per cent) of alcohol consumed was wine or fortified wine, and a slightly lower proportion (17 per cent) was spirits. Alcopops accounted for four per cent of all alcohol consumed.

In 2006, men were more likely to drink normal strength beer, lager and cider and less likely to drink strong beer, lager and cider compared with 2004, but the results were more in line with 2002. Compared with 2004, women were more likely to drink wine and less likely to drink strong beer, lager and cider and alcopops in 2006.

Where people drank last week

The most frequently mentioned place where people drank alcohol last week was at home – 46 per cent of men and 58 per cent of women had drunk alcohol in their own home in the previous week, and a further nine per cent of male drinkers and eight per cent of female drinkers had been drinking in someone else's home.

Who people drank with last week

Among men, 10 per cent had drunk alone and 36 per cent had been with one other person. A third (34 per cent) had drunk with a group of 2-5 people, and a further 20 per cent said they had been with a larger group of people. A similar pattern was found among women drinkers.

Among men who drank last week, nearly half (49 per cent) had drunk with their friends, and 45 per cent had been with a spouse or partner. Conversely, women who drank last week were more likely to have been drinking with a spouse or partner, 52 per cent, than with friends (41 per cent).

Patterns of drinking

Three tenths (30 per cent) of those interviewed said that they had drunk on at least three days a week in the last twelve months- significantly higher than in 2004 (26 per cent) but nearer to the 2002 level (32 per cent). Eleven per cent said they had had a drink almost every day in the last year. Slightly more, 13 per cent, had not drunk any alcohol at all in the last year.

Just over one quarter (24 per cent) of men had drunk more than eight units on at least one day in the previous week. The proportion who had done so fell sharply with age, ranging from 47 per cent of men aged 16-24 to just seven per cent of men aged 65 and over.

Women were much less likely than men to have drunk heavily – 12 per cent of women had drunk more than six units on at least one day in the previous week.

Note

1 The term alcopops is used to describe flavoured alcoholic drinks and pre-mixed spirits such as Hooper s Hooch, Bacardi Breezers and Smirnoff Ice, and some ciders such as Schotts Cranberry Shock Cider.

November 2006

⇨ The above information is an extract from the Office for National Statistics' report 'Drinking: adults' behaviour and knowledge in 2006' and is reprinted with permission. Visit www.statistics.gov.uk for more information.

© Crown copyright

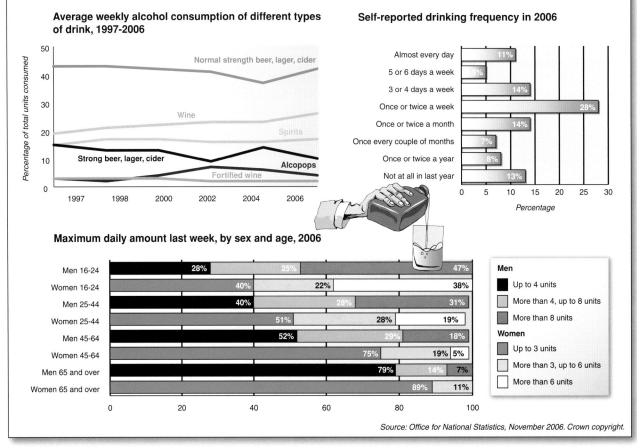

Drinking: adults' behaviour and knowledge in 2006

Statistics from Omnibus Survey Report No. 31 – *Drinking: adults' behaviour and knowledge in 2006*. A report on research using the ONS Omnibus Survey produced by the Office for National Statistics on behalf of the Information Centre for Health and Social Care.

Source: Office for National Statistics, November 2006. Crown copyright.

Binge drinking addicts

Health experts warn of English addiction to binge drinking

⇨ *A fifth of adults double safety limits once a week*
⇨ *Newcastle, Liverpool and Durham are booze capitals*

England is no longer a nation of tipplers, but a land in the grip of a dangerous alcohol addiction, public health experts warned last night after the release of research showing 18.2% of adults binge drink more than double the daily recommended limit at least once a week.

> 'Alcohol is racing ahead as one of the biggest threats to public health, not least in some of the most disadvantaged parts of the country'

In the north-east and north-west nearly a quarter of all adults consume double the limit in one or more drinking bouts each week. This is equivalent to four pints of beer or eight spirit measures in one session for men – three pints of beer, three glasses of wine or six spirit measures for women. Even in the most abstemious regions across eastern and southern England 16% of adults drink this amount or more, at least once a week.

The alcohol map was drawn up by the Centre for Public Health at Liverpool John Moores University and the North West Public Health Observatory.

It showed Newcastle, Liverpool and Durham as the capitals of binge drinking with more than 27% of adults admitting a spree at least once a week, compared with less than 10% in east Dorset.

The north-east and north-west had the most hospital admissions, with 1,100 men and 610 women admitted per 100,000 population in

By John Carvel, Social Affairs Editor

2004-05. This compared with less than 700 men and 400 women per 100,000 in the south-east.

Liverpool, Manchester and Middlesbrough had around 70% more admissions than the national average. Wokingham and West Berkshire had nearly 50% less.

Professor Mark Bellis, director of the Centre for Public Health, said: 'These profiles illustrate the growing costs of cheap alcohol, a night-time economy almost exclusively packed with bars and clubs, and a failure to deliver a credible drinking message to both youths and adults.'

Professor John Ashton, the north-west regional director of public health, blamed the government for failing to act against the drinks industry.

'Alcohol is racing ahead as one of the biggest threats to public health, not least in some of the most disadvantaged parts of the country. Fears of being accused of being part of the nanny state have intimidated governments from tackling head-on the manufacturers of cheap alcohol in the same way that they would if this was any other kind of drug.'

The average loss of life due to drinking across England was 10 months for men and five for women. But in Blackpool, men could expect to die 23 months earlier and women 13 months. In Manchester, Salford, and Barrow-in-Furness, men lost 16.5 months due to alcohol, compared with two to four months in the Isles of Scilly or east Dorset.

A spokeswoman for the Department of Health said: 'We are working hard to raise awareness and ensure that treatment is available to those who need it. The first-ever national needs assessment concerning alcohol problems has just been completed and we are getting more people into treatment.

'We are working with the drinks industry, police and health professionals to increase awareness of the dangers of excessive drinking and make sensible drinking messages easier to understand.'

But David Davis, the shadow home secretary, said: 'This alarming research shows why it was wrong of the government to unleash 24-hour drinking on all our towns and cities without a proper assessment of the consequences.'

Steve Webb, the Liberal Democrat health spokesman, said: 'The government still seems to be tiptoeing around the problem.'

4 August 2006

Binge drinking

**Young Brits are known for their heavy drinking sessions.
But what are the risks, and why do we do it?**

Are we a nation of boozers? Well, it would seem we are, we'll use any excuse to have a drink. Think of all the weddings, christenings, birthdays, Christmas parties at the office and the family gatherings, and it's always alcohol-infused. There's always one mad alcoholic auntie, dancing to Meatloaf in the living room after the funeral. Just as we find aspects of other cultures cruel and curious sometimes, is our own drinking culture sending us to an early grave?

Long term, the benefits of drinking alcohol don't apply to young people

---

I caught up with self-confessed binge drinkers Alexis Drew, 25, and Michelle Aspinall, 23, at the opening of a club. They had already tackled several cocktails by the time I caught up with them and both admitted they were dreading getting up for work in the morning, 'Going out lifts my spirits and for couple of hours I forget about the stress of work,' explains Michelle with a Long Island Ice Tea in one hand, cigarette in the other. 'Being a manager is very stressful, in the end, everything comes down to me and yoga just doesn't relax me quick enough. I work hard, why shouldn't I enjoy myself? Some people like rock climbing, I suppose I like going out and getting pissed.'

Alexis, a graphic designer agrees, 'I enjoy a sociable drink. To be honest there isn't much else to do besides go out for a drink with people you know. Yes, I appreciate there are risks involved, but so has everything. Even driving to work in the mornings I could be killed in an accident. I don't smoke or do drugs, so I figure what's wrong with a drink at the weekends. When I do go out for a

drink I know I drink too much, but that's normally just on a Friday and Saturday night.'

Medical opinion

For the science bit, we spoke to Andrew MacNeill from the Institute of Alcohol Studies: 'Short-term effects are mostly an increased risk of accidents and being the victim of an assault or attack. People often assume the assailant is under the influence but quite often it's the victim who has been drinking. It has acute effects on blood pressure and the heart rate.

Long term, the benefits of drinking alcohol don't apply to young people. 'Alcohol taken little and often can have health benefits for middle aged people but binge drinking at a young age swings this in reverse and increases the risk of heart attack. The current generation are the first ones to live this cycle and we don't really how binge drinking in your early twenties will affect them when they are older. There's been a dramatic increase in liver disease in people in their twenties, and liver transplants at such a young age aren't unheard of now.'

Socially acceptable

Crikey, liver transplants! It all sounded a bit serious so I sought a second opinion, unfortunately a spokesperson for Alcohol Concern backed up Andrew's opinion: 'In the UK we have a binge-drinking culture where drinking to get drunk is socially acceptable, especially amongst 16-24 year olds. There are both short and long term dangers linked to binge drinking.

Short-term problems include being more likely to be involved in accidents and violent incidents, poor social behaviour and unsafe sex. The Government needs to implement a National Alcohol Strategy that concentrates on prevention of harm, and tackles alcohol misuse on all fronts, offering education, public campaigns, community safety, counselling and treatment.'

⇨ The above information is re-printed with kind permission from TheSite.org. Visit www.thesite.org for more information.

© TheSite.org

Young people's drinking

Information from Alcohol Concern

Introduction

Drinking among young people is a major issue of concern for parents and people working with the young, particularly in relation to the risks of excess drinking. Rising levels of alcohol-related mortality and illness in adults also raises the question of whether problematic drinking by teenagers is a precursor for misuse in adulthood.

This article looks at the existing evidence on young people's drinking in the United Kingdom showing the prevalence of drinking, trends in drinking patterns and highlights alcohol-related problems that are specific to young people. Overall teenagers in the UK are drinking more frequently, levels of consumption are on the increase, as is binge-drinking. Increased drinking among adolescent girls is a particular matter for concern.

The focus is on young people between eleven and seventeen and aims to capture a picture of 'normal' teenage drinking behaviour.

Drinking patterns and trends

While the proportion of 11-15-year-olds who drink at all has remained at about 60% since 1988, some disturbing trends have emerged in recent years.

⇨ Among 11-15-year-olds who do drink, the average weekly consumption has doubled from 5.3 units in 1990 to 10.5 units in 2005.
⇨ Frequency of drinking has increased. The proportion of young people drinking at least once a week rose from 13% in 1990 to 17% in 2005.
⇨ The gap between young male adolescents and female adolescents has narrowed over recent years. For example the proportion of girls drinking at least once a week has risen from 12% in 1990 to 16% in 2005 compared to the proportion of boys drinking at least once a week, which rose from 15% to 17%. In addition the increase in mean consumption in girls in fractionally higher than in boys though boys still drink more. (The Information Centre, 2006)

UK teenagers report some of the highest levels of life-time drunkenness

---

⇨ Binge-drinking is common among young people in the UK. The European Schools Project survey from 2003 found that proportion of UK teenagers aged 15-16 years drinking at this level is one of the highest in Europe, with only Ireland (32%) and the Netherlands (28%) exceeding UK teenagers. Comparisons with earlier surveys in this project show that the proportion of young people who binge in the UK increased from 22% in 1995, to 30% in 1999 and then dropped back to 27% in 2004. Figures from this study also show that binge-drinking among girls overtook binge-drinking among boys with 29% of girls reporting bingedrinking 3 or more times in the last 30 days compared to 26% of boys.
⇨ UK teenagers also report some of the highest levels of life-time drunkenness – 27% report having been drunk 20 times or more in their life time. In addition 36% report being drunk at age of 13 years and they are the third highest on this scale. (Hibell, 2004)

Drinking styles

Determining styles of drinking for this age range is difficult as this is a period of transition between childhood and early adulthood. The quantitative definitions of

Current statistics on drinking (pupils aged 11-15 years)

In 2005
⇨ 58% reported ever having an alcoholic drink. The prevalence of drinking increases with age with 22% of eleven-year-olds reporting that they drank compared to 86% of 15-year-olds
⇨ 22% reported drinking in the last week
⇨ 17% said they drank at least once a week. Frequency increases with age – 37% of 15-year-olds report drinking once a week.
⇨ Among those who drink, mean alcohol consumption is 10.5 unit per week (approx.) including an average of 8.2 units among 11-year-olds and 11.8 units among 15-year-olds. (The Information Centre, 2006)
⇨ 4% of 15-16 year olds report having drunk more than 5 drinks on a single occasion in the last 30 days
⇨ 27% of this age group reported this level of drinking 3 or more times in the last 30 days. (Hibell, 2004)

'hazardous' (over 21 units a week for men and 14 units for women) and harmful drinking (over 50 units a week for men and 35 units a week for women) do not apply to teenagers and aggregate figures on consumption levels only partially describe drinking behaviour. The clearest trends in drinking patterns related to increase frequency of drinking and increased bouts of intoxication. Frequency of drinking increases with age with 2% of 12-year-olds drinking about twice a week compared to 16% of 15-year-olds. The Youth Life styles study from 1998 also found a striking increase in bouts of intoxication across ages with

22% of 12-15-year-olds reporting being very drunk in the last year compared to 63% of 16-17-year-olds. Drinking levels then tend to peak in the next age range of 16-24 years.

Newburn and Shiner in their 2001 literature review identified several stages in young people's drinking behaviour which change with increasing age:

⇨ 12-13-year-olds start tentatively experimenting with alcohol, usually within the family environment. This reflects a desire, especially in boys, to move on from child status.

⇨ 14-15-year-olds prefer to drink outside the family environment and are more secretive, hiding their behaviour from their parents. This age group tends to drink to get drunk, with the aim of testing their limits and having fun.

⇨ 16 17-year-olds move on from experimentation to seeing themselves as more responsible drinkers, with an awareness of their own limits. They are more open with their parents about drinking and see their drinking behaviour as a sign of maturity and experience by drinking similarly to adults.

⇨ Drinking is also linked to image and self-definition. Research suggests that the design, packaging and marketing of drinks appeals to young people at different ages with their different reasons for drinking. (Newburn and Shiner, 2001)

What young people drink

Many young people drink more than one type of drink and their preferences have changed slightly over the last decade

⇨ The proportion of teenagers drinking spirits and alcopops has increased over the last 10 years

⇨ There are also distinct gender differences in drink preferences, with boys more likely to drink beer, lager and cider than girls (89% of boys compared with 56% of girls). Girls are more likely to drink wine (54% compared with 33%) and alcopops (71% compared with 59%). (Information Centre, 2006)

Where young people drink

It is illegal for young people under the age of 18 to purchase alcohol and generally they cannot consume alcohol on licensed premises. However, it is not illegal for them to drink alcohol in private homes and young people are clearly able to obtain alcohol. Figure 3 shows the mostly likely drinking venues for young people.

Obtaining alcohol

The DoH 2004 survey of young people's drinking introduced a number of new questions about how young people obtained alcohol given that it is illegal for them to purchase alcohol. It found that among those who ever drank alcohol, the most common sources were parents (27%), friends (27%) bought on their behalf (20%) taken from home (18%). Stealing was rare with only 6% ever stealing from home and 1% stealing from external sources. (Bates et al., 2005)

Purchasing alcohol was unusual with 6% buying from shops (supermarkets and off-licenses) and 5% purchasing from pubs, bars or clubs. However, those who did try to purchase alcohol were often successful. The survey found that 87% of 11-15-year-olds who had tried to purchase alcohol at a pub or bar were successful as were 73% who tried to buy from a shop. Older teenagers were more successful than younger ones so 95% of 15-year-olds successfully bought alcohol compared to 64% of 11-13-year-olds. (Bates et al., 2005) The Schools Health Education Unit survey which also charts young people's behaviour, estimated that around 17% of 15-yearolds regularly purchased alcohol in 2004, with 50% being able to drink alcohol.

First drinks

It is not easy to pinpoint the actual age when young people generally first try alcohol. Recall of this event is usually vague and, as children get older, their definition of a proper drink changes. Drinkers start to outnumber non-drinkers from the age of twelve and by the age of 16 nearly all young people (94%) have tried alcohol. (Wright, 1999) Many

in this age group drink only small amounts and only occasionally, often under parental supervision. More crucial than the first drink is the age young people start to drink unsupervised, signifying a shift to drinking with friends rather than parents, and in open spaces, clubs and pubs rather than at home. A survey by the National Addiction Centre found that 65% of pupils were between 13 and 14 years old when they had their first whole alcoholic drinking without their parents knowing. (Boys, A., Farrell, M. et al., 2001)

Why do young people drink?
Motivations and influences

A recent study on young risky drinking by the Joseph Rowntree Foundation (JRF) found that the young people they interviewed cited 3 main reasons for drinking:

⇨ Social facilitation. This was the most oftenquoted motivation for drinking linking excess drinking with increased enjoyment and comfort in social situations.

⇨ Individual benefits. These were diverse and included 'escapism', getting a 'buzz' or 'something to do'.

⇨ Social norms and influences. Drinking and drinking to excess was seen as part of a wider social norm and this was linked to peer influence and one's image among peers. (Coleman and Cater, 2005)

Although this study was specifically about risky drinking patterns, the authors found that the reasons given were similar to those given in studies of more general populations of young people. (Newcombe et al. 1995, Harnett et al. 2000, Engineer et al. 2003, Brain et al. 2000) The authors argue that general samples contain a significant proportion of young people that do drink to get drunk and this is pattern of hedonistic consumption is widespread. However, they also noted some significant differences in emphasis given to individual motivation. These will be picked up in the section on problems association with alcohol misuse.

Influencing factors

Young people's attitudes and behaviour around drinking are influenced by their immediate circle of familiy, friends, and an increasing awareness of the place of alcohol in society. The most significant factors include:

⇨ Parental attitude and behaviour. Children's attitudes and behaviours are initially shaped by families – both directly, in that parents act as role models, and indirectly, in that levels of family support, control and conflict are linked to teenage drinking. (Cabinet Office, Strategy Unit, 2003) Moderate levels support and control and attitudes that support sensible drinking are thought to provide a setting that is conducive to the development of 'socially competent drinking behaviour ' in a young person. Conversely low parental support and control combined with heavy parental drinking and attitudes that condone heavy drinking are associated with excess drinking by young people. (Newburn and Shiner, 2001)

⇨ Peer group pressure. Teenage years are a time when family influences wane and the importance of external friends increases so peer pressure is often accepted as a major factor influencing drinking behaviour. However, there is also evidence pointing to a reverse phenomenon – peer association: young people who are already experimenting with certain behaviours such as using alcohol are likely to choose as friends those who share similar interests. (May, 1993)

⇨ Advertising. Young people are thought to be particularly susceptible to drinks advertising. Studies show that the more appreciative they are of advertising, the more likely they are to drink now and in the future. In addition econometric studies in the US have found that higher levels of local advertising were associated with increased binge-drinking. (Cabinet Office Strategy Unit, 2003)

⇨ Drinks retailing and marketing. Concern has been expressed over the way in which drinks are marketed to young people. After the first appearance of alcoholic lemonades and other 'alcopops' or 'ready to drink' (RTD) brands, the drinks industry focused a great deal of energy on the development of new 'designer drinks' due to their apparent appeal to the youth market. (Newburn and Shiner, 2001) Branding is a key influence and popular 'youth' brands are heavily advertised, for example £7.2 million was spent advertising Barcardi Breezer in 2002. (Cabinet Office Strategy Unit, 2003)

⇨ Price and availability. Although it is unusual for 11-15-year-olds to buy their own alcohol, survey data shows that by the age of 15 years 20% of those who drink buy alcohol from shops and 17% buy from pubs. Ease of purchase increases between the ages of 15 and 18. Despite the Home Office Alcohol Misuse Enforcement Campaign of targeted test purchasing across England and Wales, 29% of on-licensees, 21% of off-licensees and 18% of supermarkets are selling to under-18-year-olds. (Home Office, 2006)

⇨ With the improvement in household incomes over the last 30 years, alcohol has become progressively more affordable so teenagers with jobs or allowances can now purchase alcohol more easily. Research studies in the North West of England show that teenagers with a weekly income of £30 a week are twice as likely as those with £10 per week to drink frequently and in public places. (Bellis et al. 2006) As young people are sensitive to price changes there are increasing calls to either increase the real cost of alcohol, eg through taxation as proposed by Patricia Hewitt, Secretary for Health (BBC Online, 2000) in October 2006 or for parents to regulate their children's spending more rigorously. (Bellis et al 2006)

Autumn 2006

⇨ The above information is an extract from Alcohol Concern's Acquire Bulletin from Autumn 2006, and is reprinted with permission. Visit www.alcoholconcern.org.uk for more information.

© *Alcohol Concern*

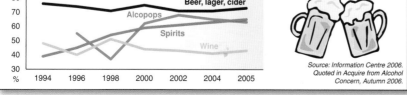

Young people and alcohol

The laws relating to young people and alcohol

Over 5 years	May consume alcohol, eg in private homes.	
Under 16 years	It is an offence to allow children under 16 onto relevant premises (premises to which a license or temporary event notice has been given) exclusively for the supply of alcohol, if they are **not** accompanied by an adult (aged 18 or over). Note that this includes every part of the premises including terraces and beer gardens.	Licensing Act 2003
Under 18 years	The legal age for purchasing alcohol is 18 years. It is an offence for: • any person to supply alcohol to children anywhere, not just on licensed premises, eg supplying smuggled alcohol from vans or car boots. • to sell alcohol to a child – unless the person charged believed he/she was 18 or over or took reasonable steps to establish the purchasers age – ie asked for proof of age identification. • it will be an offence for a child to buy or attempt to buy alcohol. • it will be an offence for a child knowingly to consume alcohol on relevant premises (see above). Exceptions: • Children aged 16-17 may drink beer, wine or cider at a table meal if they are accompanied by an adult.	Licensing Act 2003
Under 18	Police have powers to confiscate alcohol from under-18s drinking in public and to contact their parents.	Confiscation of alcohol (Young Persons) Act 1997
Under 18	When a child has been asked to test-purchase alcohol from a relevant premises by a police officer or trading standards officer. In these cases, the child will not be committing an offnce.	Licensing Act 2003

Source: Dept. for Culture, Media and Sport, 2006. Crown copyright.

Types of alcohol drunk in last seven days 1994-2005 – percentage of young people drinking a particular type of drink in the last week.

Source: Information Centre 2006. Quoted in Acquire from Alcohol Concern, Autumn 2006.

Does TV encourage teenage drinking?

Television soap operas 'normalise' alcohol consumption, de-sensitising viewers to its adverse effects and so may help to promote teenage drinking

These are the conclusions of a survey for The Food Magazine investigating the portrayal of alcohol in television soap operas. The survey discovered that alcohol, shown in background scenes or being consumed by characters, accounts for considerable screen time in many popular soaps. During the two week survey period, Hollyoaks was the leader in total alcohol related references with these accounting for around 18% of screen time. According to its website, Hollyoaks is the UK's most watched teenage drama serial; it goes out Monday to Friday at 6.30pm, right after the Simpsons.

All of the soaps surveyed go out before the 9pm watershed and have millions of viewers for each programme segment, including many children and young people. However, alcohol still plays a prominent role in these dramas.

During the survey period, the alcohol scenes in Hollyoaks were largely centred on the lives of three friends. One owned and managed a bar-restaurant while the others assisted him. The three were young twenty somethings, single, carefree and enjoying life to the full. Each looked a picture of health, of average weight and physically fit.

The characters used alcohol to help them enjoy dates and to celebrate special occasions. Even when characters were not explicitly drinking, alcohol appeared in the background – on shelves at the bar, on other tables in restaurants.

Similarly, other programmes showed characters that were exemplars of health, yet storylines showed an obvious mismatch with their unhealthy drinking habits. In Home and Away, the chief offender was a gym instructor. As might be imagined, he was fit, healthy and sporty, yet 50% of his scenes saw him drinking beer or wine. The survey showed that alcohol was the most frequent food group in background scenes, for example, 69% of all food occasions in Coronation Street involved alcohol. The chart shows how alcohol dominates the food groups appearing in background scenes of Hollyoaks.

Hollyoaks was the leader in total alcohol related references with these accounting for around 18% of screen time

---

The Food Magazine survey results are consistent with other studies. One surveyed soap opera content over several weeks and found, on average, seven drinking scenes per hour, with alcohol used primarily for celebrations and as an aid to romance. The study found no explicit portrayal of alcoholism and a tendency to portray potential problem drinkers in a humourous, or lighthearted way.

Cally Matthews, a public health nutritionist and the author of the Food Magazine report, says that the problem with over-saturation of images, particularly alcohol, is that it dulls the senses to the point in question – it becomes the 'norm'. 'Suddenly a daily lunchtime and after work visit to the pub is normal. Two to three glasses of wine each night is normal. We become desensitised to the shock of the image.'

Matthews says that evidence is accumulating about harm to young people from this 'naturalisation'. A recent study in the British Medical Journal focused on young people in the Netherlands and found that soaps were linked with alcohol abuse in young people.

The Food Magazine contacted the BBC, Channels Four and Five and ITV and received official statements confirming that they follow the Ofcom Broadcasting Code, with, for example, Channel 5 asserting, 'Representation of alcohol use and/or abuse in Five programming is governed by the guidelines laid down by the Ofcom Broadcasting Code. In accordance with these, alcohol is not featured in programmes made primarily for children unless there

Pupils who drank alcohol in the last week

Proportion of pupils who drank alcohol in the last week, by age: 1988-2006

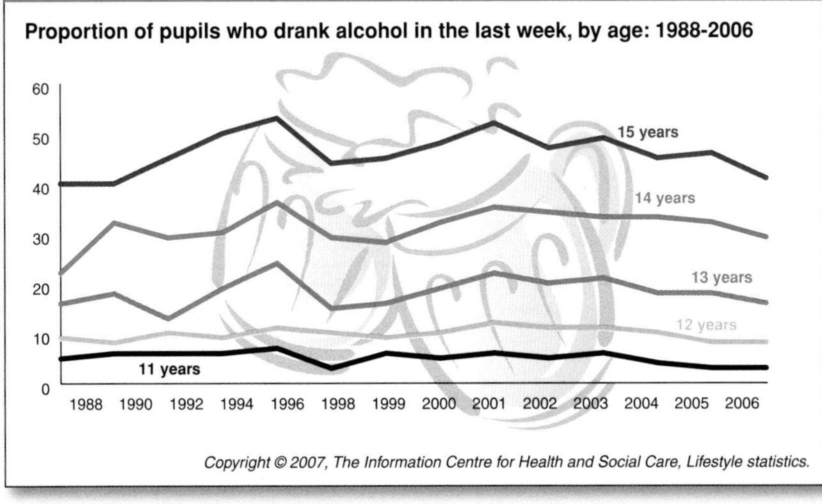

Copyright © 2007, The Information Centre for Health and Social Care, Lifestyle statistics.

is strong editorial justification. In other programmes broadcast before the watershed which are likely to be viewed widely by under eighteens, alcohol abuse is generally avoided, and in any case not condoned, encouraged or glamourised unless there is editorial justification.'

As the soaps surveyed all have bars or clubs or pubs as significant settings, it is likely that 'editorial justification' is going to allow many scenes with alcohol. The questions of glamourisation and encouragement are perhaps more open to interpretation. The regulator, Ofcom, is charged with enforcing its Code, but day to day programme content is more likely to be monitored, and complained about, by members of the public who object to certain scenes.

Cally Matthews argues that while the nation's soaps continue the process of normalisation of alcohol under the watchful gaze of the regulator, campaigners have focused their attention on efforts to get a pre-9pm watershed ban on alcohol advertising on television.

The drinks industry spends around £800 million a year promoting its products, against a spend last year by the government of not quite £4 million on safe drinking campaigns. Campaigners want to make sure young people are protected as much as possible from the power of that spend and believe a total pre-9pm ban is the best way to do this.

A recent study, published in the Archives of Pediatrics and Adolescent Medicine, found that young people aged 15-26 who watched more alcohol adverts tended to drink more too. Nearly 2000 young people were interviewed for the study, which took place in the United States.

Scheduling restrictions on TV advertisements are almost all based on the Broadcasters Audience Research Board audience index. Programmes attract alcohol advertising restrictions if the proportion of under 18s in the audience is greater than the proportion of under 18s in the population at large.

This still leaves some programmes with many young viewers but not of a high enough percentage to enact a

ban; it also means that programmes with very high overall viewing figures need large child audiences to enact a ban. For example, alcohol adverts are allowed during Home and Away – a programme full of young characters that goes out on weekdays at noon and 6pm and which has a viewing audience comprised of around 8% under 16 year olds.

The complexities of the current system mean that it is not that easy to find out if advertising is allowed during specific programmes. The Advertising Standards Authority (ASA) was unable to tell The Food Magazine whether alcohol adverts were allowed during Emmerdale, Coronation Street, Hollyoaks and Home and Away, despite its role as a so-called one-stop-shop for consumers concerned about advertisements. They advised asking the Broadcast Advertising Clearance Centre (BACC), a specialist body responsible for the pre-transmission examination and clearance of television advertisements.

However, BACC said, 'Our role is to advise broadcasters of the character of the commercial, and in this case, we will inform the broadcaster whether it is a commercial for alcohol. It is up to the broadcaster to apply the scheduling restrictions which apply, and they are therefore better placed to reply to your question, whether the four programmes have a higher share of young among their viewership.'

The Food Magazine checked back with the ASA which responded that they work on a complaints basis; if the Food Magazine had a complaint about a specific alcohol advert they

would then investigate and the broadcasters would have to release audience information to them.

Cally Matthews argues that this type of system calls into question the degree of regulation and is not particularly useful to a parent who might not want to sit and watch a programme, but who would prefer to find out if adverts for alcohol were likely to occur during programmes their children would be watching. The Food Magazine tried to get in touch with, for example, Channel 4 and were told that it could take up to three weeks for an answer.

According to Jane Landon, Deputy Chief Executive of the National Heart Forum, 'A pre-9pm watershed ban is logical, it is easy for people to monitor at home, as all they need to do is look at their watch to see if an advert is on when it shouldn't be. A watershed also offers a higher protection to all children and young people, as we know many young people watch all kinds of programmes which attract a mixed audience. At the moment the viewer at home is left to decide whether to make a complaint, which is then investigated by the Advertising Standards Authority. Even if at a later date the ASA rules against a broadcaster, the consequence is usually the regulatory equivalent of a slap on the wrist.'

Issue 76 of The Food Magazine, 10 March 2007

⇨ The above information is reprinted with kind permission from the Institute for Alcohol Studies. Visit www.ias.org.uk for more information.

Children and alcohol

Alcohol consumption amongst children reaches new heights

The amount of alcohol consumed by girls aged between 11-13 has increased by 82.6% between 2000-2006, while for boys the number has gone up by 43.4% during the same period. These startling findings, which are just one of a series of worrying developments are published in a new report from Alcohol Concern entitled Glass Half Empty? The report offers a wide-ranging assessment of the impact of the Governments Alcohol Harm Reduction Strategy.

> The amount of alcohol consumed by girls aged between 11-13 has increased by 82.6% between 2000-2006

Srabani Sen, Chief Executive of Alcohol Concern, says:

Binge drinking by children can have serious consequences for brain function, significantly raises the risk of alcohol dependency in later life and diminishes their life chances. Our report shows that we are simply not doing enough to protect our children from alcohol.

Alcohol Concern recommends limiting the access children and teenagers have to alcohol and challenging more aggressively the drivers of underage consumption:

Make it illegal to provide alcohol to anyone under the age of 15. Currently it is legal to provide children as young as five with alcohol in a private home. Raising the age limit to fifteen would send a stronger message to parents of the risks associated with letting very young people consume alcohol.

Enforce the law around underage purchase. Data from the most recent Home Office AMEC (test purchasing) campaign showed that 29% of underage participants were able to buy alcohol in pubs and bars, while 21% did so successfully in off-licenses. Local police forces and trading standard units must devote more resources to identifying and prosecuting those outlets in breach of the law.

End advertising of alcohol on TV before the watershed and in cinemas when films with ratings below 18 are shown. The European Court of Justice has already refuted advertisers arguments and ruled, It is in fact undeniable that advertising acts as an encouragement to consumption. Alcohol Concerns report shows that supermarket alcohol promotions were shown twice as often before 9pm (which is when children are more likely to be watching TV) compared to after. Furthermore, 82% of films shown in cinemas featuring alcohol adverts have ratings of 15 or below.

Make alcohol education part of the National Curriculum. Inappropriate use of alcohol by young people has been shown to have an impact on school performance. Alcohol is a factor in many school exclusions and suspensions. Around 14% of pupils excluded from school were suspended for drinking alcohol at school. The PSHE components of the National Curriculum should provide an important opportunity for conveying to young people the risks associated with bingeing.

Copies of Glass Half-Empty (under embargo) are available from the Alcohol Concern website.
27 April 2007

⇨ The above information is reprinted with kind permission from Alcohol Concern. Visit wwwalcoholconcern.org.uk for more information.
© *Alcohol Concern*

Alcohol and adolescence

Information from Alcoweb

Alcohol and the young in Europe

Some general trends in alcohol consumption by the young can be observed in Europe. In most countries of northern Europe, such as Holland, Finland, Ireland and especially Poland, the frequency and quantities consumed have increased during the last 10 years. On the other hand, consumption of alcohol by the young has stabilised, and sometimes even decreased, in countries such as France, Italy and Norway.

Alcohol consumption varies from one country to another, depending on:
⇨ the national context of alcohol consumption and the influence of advertising
⇨ the role of the family environment
⇨ relationships between young people

⇨ the social importance of alcohol
⇨ the importance of initiation and regular consumption

First drinks

Among 11-15 year olds, six out of 10 young Europeans, 65% of boys and 57% of girls, have tasted an alcoholic drink. Initiation is early: one of every four Europeans, 28% of boys and 21% of girls, admit to having drunk their first drinks before the age of 11 years. Three alcoholic beverages are the most common routes of access to alcohol consumption: beer (37% of young Europeans say that the first alcohol they consumed was beer), wine (24%) and champagne (21%).

Regular consumption

Nearly 14% of young Europeans consume alcohol regularly (at least once a week). These are always from the same countries that have highest regular alcohol consumption. This increases very significantly with age. At 15 years, 31% of boys and 19% of girls are regular consumers of alcohol; they drink alcohol at least once a week. The drink consumed most often by adolescents is beer; this is true whatever the country. Between 18 and 24 years of age, regular consumption is widespread.

Intoxication

Around 33% of young Europeans aged 15 years say that they have been drunk during the last 6 months.

⇨ The above information is reprinted with kind permission from Alcoweb. Visit www.alcoweb.com for more information.

© Alcoweb

How dangerous is alcohol?

Alcohol worse than ecstasy on shock new drug list

Some of Britain's leading drug experts demand today that the government's classification regime be scrapped and replaced by one that more honestly reflects the harm caused by alcohol and tobacco. They say the current ABC system is 'arbitrary' and not based on evidence.

The scientists, including members of the government's top advisory committee on drug classification, have produced a rigorous assessment of the social and individual harm caused by 20 substances, and believe this should form the basis of any future ranking.

By their analysis, alcohol and tobacco are rated as more dangerous than cannabis, LSD and ecstasy.

They say that if the current ABC system is retained, alcohol would be rated a class A drug and tobacco class B.

By James Randerson, Science Correspondent

'We face a huge problem,' said Colin Blakemore, chief executive of the Medical Research Council and an author of the report, which is published in the Lancet medical journal. 'Drugs ... have never been more easily available, have never been cheaper, never been more potent and never been more widely used.

'The policies we have had for the last 40 years ... clearly have not worked in terms of reducing drug use. So I think it does deserve a fresh look. The principal objective of this study was to bring a dispassionate approach to what is a very passionate issue.'

David Nutt, a psychopharmacologist at Bristol University and

member of the Advisory Council on Misuse of Drugs (ACMD) which advises ministers on drug policy, added: 'What we are trying to say is we should review the penalties in the light of the harms and try to have a more proportionate legal response.

Some experts claim alcohol is more dangerous than many illegal substances

'The point we are making is that all drugs are dangerous, even the ones that people know and love and use regularly like alcohol.'

Professor Nutt and his team analysed the evidence of harm caused by 20 drugs including heroin, cocaine, cannabis, ecstasy, LSD and tobacco.

'All drugs are dangerous, even the ones that people know and love and use regularly like alcohol.'

They asked a group of 29 consultant psychiatrists who specialise in addiction to rate the drugs in nine categories. Three of these related to physical harm, three to the likelihood of addiction and three to social harms such as healthcare costs. The team also extended the analysis to another group of 16 experts spanning several fields including chemistry, pharmacology, psychiatry, forensics, police and legal services.

The final rankings placed heroin and cocaine as the most dangerous of the 20 drugs. Alcohol was fifth, the class C drug ketamine sixth and tobacco was in ninth place, just behind amphetamine or 'speed'.

Cannabis was 11th, while LSD and ecstasy were 14th and 18th respectively. The rankings do take into account new evidence that specially cultivated 'skunk' varieties of cannabis available now are two to

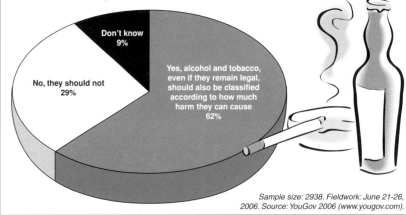

Classification of legal drugs

Respondents were asked: 'At the moment different illegal drugs are classified from A to C, roughly according to how much harm they are thought to cause individuals and society. For the guidance of the public, do you think different alcoholic drinks and different forms of tobacco should be classified according to how much harm they can cause?'

Don't know 9%

No, they should not 29%

Yes, alcohol and tobacco, even if they remain legal, should also be classified according to how much harm they can cause 62%

Sample size: 2938. Fieldwork: June 21-26, 2006. Source: YouGov 2006 (www.yougov.com).

three times stronger than traditional cannabis resin.

Evan Harris MP, the Liberal Democrats' science spokesman, said the paper undermines the government's claim that drug policy is evidence-based. 'This comes from the top echelons of the government's own advisory committee on the misuse of drugs. It blows a hole in the government's current classification system for drugs.' He said the ACMD should make recommendations to ministers on how to change drug policy based on the findings.

But the shadow home secretary, David Davis, rejected any changes that would confuse the public. 'Drugs wreck lives, destroy communities and fuel other sorts of crime – especially gun and knife crime. Thanks to the government's chaotic and confused approach to drugs policy, young

people increasingly think it is OK to take drugs,' he said, adding that he was against downgrading of ecstasy. 'It is vital nothing else leads young people to believe drugs are OK.'

The position of ecstasy near the bottom of the list was defended by Prof Nutt, who said that apart from some tragic isolated cases ecstasy is relatively safe. Despite about a third of young people having tried the drug and around half a million users every weekend, it causes fewer than 10 deaths a year. One person a day is killed by acute alcohol poisoning and thousands more from chronic use.

Prof Nutt said young people already know ecstasy is relatively safe, so having it in class A makes a mockery of the entire classification system for them. 'The whole harm-reduction message disappears because people say, 'They are lying.' Let's treat people as adults, tell them the truth and hopefully work with them to minimise use.'

Another advantage of the new system, according to Professor Blakemore, is that it would be easy to tweak the rankings based on new evidence.

The public furore over the downgrading of cannabis from B to C, he said, showed how hard it is to change drug classifications once they are fixed. '[Our system] would be easy to use on a rolling basis, to reassess the harms of drugs as evidence developed,' he said.

23 March 2007

© Guardian Newspapers Limited 2007

No, I don't do drugs!

Crime and licensing hours

Serious violence injuries down despite licensing hours change

Serious violence-related injuries fell by 2% in England and Wales last year, despite the change in pub opening hours, according to a new Cardiff University study.

This year's annual violence study, by the University's Violence Research Group, is the first complete set of data since the licensing laws changed in November 2005. The law change triggered fears that longer opening hours would see a rise in street violence. However, the Cardiff researchers found that approximately 6,000 fewer people needed hospital treatment for violence injuries than in 2005.

The Cardiff researchers analysed data for 2006 from 33 Accident and Emergency departm ents across England and Wales. The 2% fall is less dramatic than in previous years and the figure for violence against men was unchanged. However, there was a sharp 8% drop in the number of female victims.

As in previous years, the study found violence rates were highest at weekends. There were more incidents between April and October, peaking in July.

The Research Group study was set up to complement official Home Office statistics (also published today). The Cardiff study has shown a consistent fall in the number of assault victims since 2000, while violent incidents recorded by the police have risen.

Professor Jonathan Shepherd, director of the Violence Research Group, said: 'It seems likely that street CCTV and better targeted patrols mean that police are getting to fights more often and earlier. This would explain why incident numbers are up and injuries are down – police are intervening before anyone is seriously hurt. This illustrates the increasing injury prevention benefits of CCTV and targeted police activity in city centres.

'We estimate that some 364,000 people needed hospital treatment for assaults last year. That is still too many, but it is encouraging to see that the trend is downwards and that the feared effect of the licensing law change has not materialised.'
26 April 2007

⇨ The above information is reprinted with kind permission from Cardiff University. Visit www.cardiff. ac.uk for more information.
© Cardiff University

Drink-driving

Information from Brake

11 people are killed by drink drivers on uk roads every week.

These deaths can be stopped if all drivers pledge never to drink and drive – not even a drop.

The effects of alcohol

Alcohol is a depressant drug and even small amounts of alcohol (such as half a pint of lager) affect drivers' reaction times, judgment and coordination. Alcohol also makes it impossible for drivers to assess their own impairment because it creates a false sense of confidence and means drivers are more inclined to take risks and believe they are in control when they are not. For these reasons, the only way for drivers to be safe is to not drink anything at all before driving.

It is also impossible to calculate how much alcohol you have in your blood (even if you know exactly how much you have consumed), or how

Brake
the road safety charity
www.brake.org.uk

long it will stay in your system. The speed at which alcohol is absorbed into your system (and how quickly your system gets rid of it) depends on a large number of factors, including your sex, weight, metabolism, health and when you last ate.

There's no way of knowing exactly how long it takes to sober up completely after drinking, but it's probably longer than you think. For example, if you finish your fourth pint of normal strength beer at 11pm, you probably won't be sober until 10am the next day – but it could take much longer.

Drinking coffee, eating, sleeping and showering don't make you sober up any faster. It just takes time.
⇨ Never drink any amount of alcohol if you're driving
⇨ Never drink if you're driving early the next morning
⇨ Take responsibility for others – never buy a drink for someone who is driving
⇨ Tell your employer immediately (and in confidence) if you catch acolleague drink-driving – for their own safety and that of other road users

The fight against drink-driving goes on

Drink-drive casualties (deaths, serious injuries and minor injuries) decreased significantly during the 1980s, but rose by nearly a third between 1993 and 2002 (from 14,980 to 20,140). Drink-drive deaths account for one in six road deaths.[1]

These Government statistics only include casualties caused by drivers over the drink-drive limit, yet many more drink-drive crashes are caused by drivers who only have small amounts of alcohol in their blood. An estimated 80 road deaths per year are caused by drivers who are under the drink-drive limit, but who have a significant amount of alcohol in their blood.[2]

The current drink-drive limit in the UK is 80mg of alcohol per 100ml of blood, significantly higher than the majority of EU countries

---

According to a survey of 1,000 drivers by Brake, the road safety charity, half of drivers admit to drink-driving (after drinking any amount of alcohol at least once in the last twelve months), and one in four drivers admit to driving after drinking an amount of alcohol they know is affecting their driving.[3]

More than one in four drivers (28%) also admit driving the morning after having a lot to drink, when they are likely to still be over the limit.[4]

Alcohol use as a whole is estimated to cost UK companies approximately £700 million a year, with between eight and 14 million working days lost each year due to alcohol use. [5]

The worst offenders

Certain types of driver are more likely to drink-drive than others:

⇨ Occupational drivers – in Brake's survey of 1,000 drivers, drivers who drive for work were more likely to admit drink-driving (driving after drinking any amount of alcohol, at least once in the previous twelve months) than other drivers (57% compared to 43%).[6]

⇨ Car drivers – are most likely to fail a breath test, followed by motorbike riders.[7]

⇨ Young drivers – drivers age 17-24 have the highest level of drink-drive crashes per distance travelled.[8]

⇨ Male drivers – 89% of convictions for dangerous driving while under the influence of alcohol in 2002 were men.[9]

The risks

Drink-driving puts both drivers and other road users at risk. Of the 20,060 people killed or injured in drink-drive crashes in 2002 there were:

⇨ 740 pedestrians, including 120 children;

⇨ 140 cyclists, including 40 children;

⇨ 6,930 car passengers, including 850 children;

⇨ 720 passengers in other vehicles, including 40 children;

⇨ plus many drivers and motor cyclists who had not been drinking themselves but were hit by drink-drivers.[10]

At twice the legal limit, drivers are at least 50 times more likely to be involved in a fatal crash. [11]

The law – the drink-drive limit

The current drink-drive limit in the UK is 80mg of alcohol per 100ml of blood, significantly higher than the majority of EU countries (the EC recommends a limit of 50mg of alcohol per 100ml of blood or less). Research shows that a driver's judgement and motor skills are affected when they are still well below the legal alcohol limit.[12]

An estimated 80 people die each year in crashes caused by drivers who are impaired by alcohol but who are under the limit. [13]

Charges and penalties

If a driver is found to be either over the drink-drive limit, and/or driving while impaired by alcohol, they can receive a maximum penalty of six months in prison and an unlimited fine. Anyone convicted must also receive a one-year disqualification. If a driver kills someone while under the influence of alcohol, they can be charged with death by careless driving while under the influence of drink or drugs, which carries a maximum penalty of fourteen years in prison.

Remember: never drink any amount of alcohol if you're driving.

1 Road Casualties Great Britain 2003: Annual Report (Department for Transport, 2004)

2 Drinking and driving fact sheet (Institute of Alcohol Studies, 2004)

3 The Green Flag Report on Safe Driving 2004: Part one, Fit to Drive? (Brake, 2004)

4 The Green Flag Report on Safe Driving 2004: Part one, Fit to Drive? (Brake, 2004)

5 Alcohol and the workplace (Institute of Alcohol Studies, 2003)

6 The Green Flag Report on Safe Driving 2004: Part one, Fit to Drive? (Brake, 2004)

7 Road Casualties Great Britain 2003: Annual Report (Department for Transport, 2004)

8 Road Casualties Great Britain 2003: Annual Report (Department for Transport, 2004)

9 Motoring Offences and Breath Test Statistics – England and Wales 2002 (Home Office)

10 Road Casualties Great Britain 2003: Annual Report (Department for Transport, 2004)

11 Think! Road Safety campaign, www.thinkroadsafety.co.uk (Department for Transport)

12 Think! Road Safety campaign, www.thinkroadsafety.co.uk (Department for Transport)

13 Drinking and driving fact sheet (Institute of Alcohol Studies, 2004)

⇨ The above information is reprinted with kind permission from Brake. Visit www.brake.org.uk for more information.

© *Brake*

Frequently asked questions about alcohol

Information from the Addiction Recovery Agency

What is a safe amount to drink?

The recommended amount for adults is:

⇨ Women: 14 units a week (1-2 units a day)

⇨ Men: 21 units a week (1-3 units a day)

These units are for people whose bodies are fully developed. Therefore a young person should be drinking less than the amount recommended for adults. There are no safe limits set for young people.

I can't be a problem drinker because…

…I'm not a down and out

Many think of problem drinkers as 'down and outs', as people who have no self respect, position or future. This may be true for some but it is also true that many people are leading apparently 'ordinary lives', many of whom still have good jobs, are maintaining their families, and are 'getting along' but they often have a difficult time of it because of drinking. Many do not realise themselves that they have a problem, although they may be beginning to experience not feeling well, or not handling matters as well as they want.

…I never drink before 5.00pm

Some people have the mistaken idea that no one is an alcoholic unless she/he has to have a drink in the morning. This is not true. It is true that the need for a 'morning drink' is one of the symptoms of the chronic stage of alcoholism. But simply because one does not crave a drink in the morning does not mean that one is not an alcoholic. You may be able to wait all day for a drink but when it comes you find you drink much more that you intended and

have felt tense during the day until the 'time' for your drink approaches. You may well have a problem. It is not when you drink but whether you can control the amount you drink that determines whether you have a drink problem. If your partner starts insisting you have a drink problem this may indeed be true.

…I never drink anything but beer

This is a fallacy. Each half a pint of ordinary beer has the same amount of alcohol as a pub measure of spirit or a small glass of wine, this amount is referred to as one unit of alcohol. All alcohol has to be burned up by the liver before eventually leaving the body and each unit of alcohol takes up to one hour to do this. So every pint of beer drunk will take about two hours for the liver to process and the body to be cleared of alcohol.

…I'm too young

Some people seem to drink heavily for many years before any harm is noticed. It is not your age or how many years you have been drinking but what alcohol is doing to you. Loss of control can occur anytime in a person's drinking history. Women are particularly at risk as their bodies do not tolerate as much alcohol as men.

If you think you have a problem…

If you feel you have a problem do seek help. You may feel that you will never be able to control the alcohol or even admit you have a problem, but the problem will get progressively worse if you do not face up to it. It is a fact that other people have asked for help and found the situation can be resolved. If you DO want to stop, there is help available. Contact your local Alcohol Advisory Centre, who will

be able to give you information and counselling if requested, and can also give information about other helping agencies eg. Alcoholics Anonymous.

What exactly is counselling?

Counselling is a kind of help. It provides an opportunity for you to talk things through with someone who will listen to you carefully and sympathetically, and who will not judge you in thinking of ways to solve your problems or to live with them.

How can I help a relative with a drinking problem?

Talk to the person you're worried about. Find a time when they're sober and when you're both reasonably calm. Tell them about the problems their drinking is causing. Listen to them. Find out how they feel about their drinking, and how it helps them. Discuss with other members of the family what you are trying to do. This will make it easier for everyone to take a similar approach, and it will be less confusing to the person who is drinking.

Should I drink if I'm pregnant?

It can be dangerous to drink too much during pregnancy as alcohol passes through the placenta into the foetal bloodstream. If you are planning to become pregnant it is a good idea to start thinking about your alcohol intake a couple of months in advance.

Safe limits of drinking when pregnant: 1-2 units per week.

⇨ Information from the Addiction Recovery Agency. Visit www.addictionrecovery.org.uk for more information.

© Addiction Recovery Agency

Questions and answers on responsible drinking

Information from the Portman Group

Responsible drinking' – isn't that a contradiction in terms?
Don't be misled by the bad image alcohol sometimes attracts. Like air travel, it only hits the headlines when something goes wrong. Alcohol misuse is a problem for a minority. The majority of those who drink do so responsibly.

Units are a way of measuring how much alcohol you're drinking. A unit is 8 grams of pure alcohol

---

Isn't it a bit dreary though?
Thanks to research studies, we now know much more about how to drink in a way that is compatible with a healthy lifestyle. We also know more about the health and other risks we run if we ignore that information. So 'responsible drinking' is a way of enjoying the pleasure and the benefits, but avoiding the hazards and the harm.

Is it true the Government has put up my weekly alcohol allowance?
No! The latest guidelines abolish weekly limits altogether. Instead, they give us daily benchmarks.

So what's a daily benchmark?
It's the amount of alcohol that the Government's Responsible Drinking guidelines say that most people can drink in a day without putting your health at risk. But it's a guide, not a target.

So I could still take it easy during the week and use up my 'allowance' on Saturday night?
No again. Since the old guidelines (which used to give weekly limits), new research has shown how harmful 'binge drinking' can be. There's a world of difference between drinking, say, a pint of beer or a glass of wine every day, and going without during the week just to get plastered on 7 pints or a whole bottle of wine on Saturday night. It's not just the amount, it's how you spread it out that counts.

So how much is OK to drink each day?
That depends on whether you're male or female. Most men are OK for 3 to 4 units a day, most women for 2 to 3. But if men consistently drink 4 or more units a day, the health risks start to accumulate. The same goes for women who consistently drink 3 or more units a day.

Units? What on earth are units?
Units are a way of measuring how much alcohol you're drinking. A unit is 8 grams of pure alcohol, if you want to be scientific about it. But the amount of alcohol in any given type of drink will obviously depend on how big the glass, can or bottle is, and how strong the drink is.

I'm no Einstein. How can I keep track of my units without being a whiz-kid at maths?
Luckily, most drinks come in fairly standard sizes and strengths. So it's quite easy to keep an accurate enough tally – if you're drinking out, that is. If you're having spirits or wine at home, though, you'll need to be more alert, as you can bet you'll be helping yourself to larger servings than the pub or restaurant would give you! The examples in The Portman Group's leaflet 'It all adds up' give the most workable unit ranges, to the nearest half-unit, for the most common drinks in the most common servings. You could use that as a ready reckoner.

Can you give me some 'rule of thumb' examples?
Sure: half a pint of ordinary strength beer is 1 unit. A single pub measure of spirits is also 1 unit. A small glass of 11% ABV wine is 1.5 units.

How would I work all this out for myself?
If you want to do the arithmetic accurately yourself, the formula is to multiply the amount of liquid

(volume), measured in mls, by the alcoholic strength, measured in percentage ABV. Then you divide the total by 1000 to get the number of units. Some drinks have unit information on the label, to save you the trouble.

Surely different people can tolerate different amounts of alcohol?
Of course there are individual differences. Some people shouldn't drink at all. Children under 16 should not assume these guidelines apply to them either, as their bodies have not yet matured enough to deal with alcohol in the same way as adults. But the scientific research on which the guidelines are based does enable advice to be given both to men in general and women in general.

Are there any other exceptions to the rule?
People involved in certain activities where safety and control are paramount are advised not to drink at all. Driving is an obvious one. Before swimming or other active physical sports is another no-go area for drinking. And you shouldn't drink if you're about to operate machinery, go up ladders or do any kind of work which requires you to have your wits fully about you. Taking certain medications is also incompatible with drinking alcohol.

Why shouldn't women drink as much as men?
A woman drinking the same amount as a man of exactly the same size will get intoxicated faster because she has a lower proportion of water in her body weight. This leads to a higher concentration of alcohol in the body tissue. Women's average weight is lower than men's in any case. And just for good measure, the scientists also think that women's bodies break alcohol down more slowly than men's, so alcoholic drink has a longer-lasting effect.

Is it OK to drink in pregnancy?
If you're pregnant – or planning to be – then you've got to be sensible for two. The guidelines say that no more than 1 or 2 units once or twice a week should be the benchmark for you. Drunkenness should also

be avoided, which should be easy enough if you're sticking to those guidelines.

I thought drinking red wine every day was supposed to be good for your heart. There must be some good news in here somewhere...?
Well, the reference to red wine is a bit of a red herring. The good news is that it's any kind of alcohol, not just wine or red wine, that can have a significant protective effect on your heart. The bad news for all you strapping young twenty- or thirty-somethings out there is that the health benefit only kicks in for men over 40 and for women after the menopause.

A woman drinking the same amount as a man of exactly the same size will get intoxicated faster

---

Does that mean we can drink more as we get older?
Afraid not. It's important to remember that the maximum health advantage for the heart for men over 40 and women past the menopause comes from drinking between 1 and 2 units a day. Drinking more doesn't increase the benefit.

Why should I believe anything the Government advises?
The Government didn't just pluck the figures out of the air. The advice in the guidelines was drawn up after considering 89 written submissions, 43 of which came from scientific, academic or medical sources; 21 from the health promotion field and service providers, 9 from the drinks industry and 16 others.

It's all so complicated. Wouldn't it just be easier – and more honest – to get everyone to drink less?
Some people believe that if less alcohol were consumed by the population as a whole, there would be fewer alcohol-related problems. But this doesn't necessarily follow. Take the example of deaths caused by drink-driving in the UK. The

numbers have dropped dramatically without the overall level of alcohol consumption going down. This has been achieved because people have responded positively to well-communicated messages about their behaviour. By the same token, people are more likely to continue drinking responsibly, or begin to drink responsibly, if they are informed by a general public health message which they can interpret in relation to their own personal behaviour and choices. They don't want to feel punished or guilty or nagged because of other people's over-indulgence, when they are doing no harm to their own health.

Are you seriously telling me that the drinks industry supports sensible drinking. What's in it for them?
You could put that the other way round: what's in it for the drinks industry if it does nothing about the way a minority of people misuse its products? The major alcoholic drinks companies set up The Portman Group in 1989 because they were genuinely committed to promoting responsible drinking and helping to prevent alcohol abuse. Our policies and work are carried out irrespective of the commercial consequences to the industry.

But they wouldn't fund The Portman Group if you weren't helping the industry, would they?
Exactly, and we believe that promoting responsible drinking, as well as being a worthwhile activity in its own right, is also in the long term interests of the industry. Call it enlightened self-interest. If consumers and the industry can both benefit from the same approach, perhaps being sensible is not such a dreary idea after all. Being responsible and getting pleasure are not mutually exclusive activities. Responsible drinking is one way to do both.

⇨ The above information is re-printed with kind permission from the Portman Group. Visit www.portman-group.org.uk for more information.

© *Portman Group*

Tackling underage drinking

Alcohol industry must do more to tackle underage sales

The Government today urged the alcohol industry to do more to stop the sale of alcohol to children as new figures show that, despite recent progress, too much of the licensed trade is still illegally selling alcohol to under 18s.

The figures from the fourth Alcohol Misuse Enforcement Campaign (AMEC) show that nearly one in three minors taking part in trading standards operations were able to buy alcohol in bars and pubs, and one in five were able to buy alcohol in off-licences.

The test purchase results show widespread variation between individual companies and regions. For example, on-licence premises in Wales sold alcohol to 48 per cent of young people taking part in test purchases, while those in the North East sold to 18 per cent.

Home Office Minister Vernon Coaker and Department for Culture, Media and Sport Minister Shaun Woodward met with representatives of the licensed trade industry this week to discuss the results of the Government's fourth campaign to clamp down on alcohol related disorder.

Home Office Minister Vernon Coaker said:

'I am disappointed with these test purchase results. The problem of alcohol fuelled crime and disorder is an issue of major public concern and we are all responsible for tackling it.

'We have given police new powers, such as fixed penalty notices, to deal with alcohol related disorder. However the licensed trade need to build on the real progress they have made to drive down sales to young people even further. I am heartened by the industry's assurances that they are committed to achieving this but I have made it clear to them that we expect to see real improvements in their performance. I will continue to monitor the situation to ensure this happens.'

Licensing Minister at the Department for Culture, Media and Sport Shaun Woodward said:

'Too many supermarkets, bars, clubs and pubs continue to sell alcohol to under 18s. This is not acceptable.

'We've given police and local authorities tough new powers to deal with premises that break the law – if you sell alcohol to children you face having your licence revoked or a £5,000 fine.'

The results also show that the police continued to clamp down on alcohol related disorder, visiting over 30,000 licensed premises and issuing 7,300 fixed penalty notices.

Mike Craik, ACPO lead on alcohol issues and Chief Constable of Northumbria Police said:

'Taking firm action against retailers who flout the law by selling alcohol to young people, will help the rest of us to enjoy responsible 'grown-up' drinking without fear of our socialising being ruined by drunken louts.

'The message to retailers is loud and clear; flout the law by selling to those underage and you can expect to be hit financially through a suspension or revocation of your premises license.

'This campaign demonstrates the good work of police officers who are working hard to clamp down on irresponsible retailers. We will continue to develop the strategy of this campaign into mainstream policing so we can build public trust and confidence in our ability to tackle alcohol related disorder throughout the rest of the year.'

Representatives of both the on-licence and off-licence industries had constructive discussions with Ministers at meetings this week to look at the measures they were taking forward to build on the substantial progress already made.

Rob Hayward, Chief Executive of the British Beer and Pub Association (BBPA), said:

'BBPA and the British Entertainment and Dance Association (BEDA) are fully committed to working closely with the Government to reduce underage sales. Progress has been made in bringing down test purchase failures from 45 per cent to 29 per cent since summer 2005. However, we recognise that more needs to be done.

'Companies are tackling these issues head on, by developing new and innovative ways of ensuring managers, licensees, bar staff and the public are aware of our determination to tackle underage sales.

'Our Challenge 21 poster campaign, designed to raise awareness of the critical nature of ID checking, continues to gather pace with more than 180,000 posters issued to venues across the country. In May, we discussed with Government new initiatives, which will target not just underage sales, but a host of other drinks retailing standards. We expect to see the results of these initiatives coming through in future test purchase figures.'

Nick Grant, Chair of the Retail of Alcohol Standards Group, commented:

'We're pleased the trend is very much going in the right direction.

'The Retail of Alcohol Standards Group (RASG) has achieved an enormous amount since it was formed a year ago. Test purchase failure rates have fallen from 36 per cent to 21 per cent for the 'off-trade' in general and from 50 per cent to 18 per cent for supermarkets in particular.

'Members are committed to tackling under age sales. They devote considerable resources to measures including staff training, research, IT and public information and, clearly, there's more to do. This is about delivering long-term, lasting results and we are confident we can bring the failure rate down even further.'

18 October 2006

⇨ The above information is reprinted with kind permission from the Home Office. Visit www.drugs.gov.uk for more information.

Raise drinking age to 21, says think tank

It says measure needed to tackle binge drinking

Young people should be banned from drinking until they reach 21 or be forced to carry a card that records their alcohol intake, a think tank columnist claims today.

Binge drinking has become such an 'overwhelming' problem, argues the journal of the left-leaning Institute for Public Policy Research, that policy makers need to practice 'tough love' and put drink out of the reach of youngsters.

In an article to be published this week columnist Jasper Gerard will say that the UK has 'lost the plot' over drinking laws.

He proposes raising the drinking age to 21 or requiring 18-year-olds to carry smart cards which record how much they have drunk each night and restricting them to three units of alcohol.

Binge drinking

Gerrard will also propose increasing the number of prosecutions and the level of fines on retailers selling alcohol to under-age drinkers and upping taxes on alcopops

He said: 'The adverse social effects of binge drinking are now so overwhelming that we need to practice tough love.

'By raising the age threshold it is at least possible that those in their early and mid teens will not see drink as something they will soon be allowed to do so therefore they might as well start doing it surreptitiously now. Instead they might come to see it as it should be: forbidden.'

The number of under-18s taken to hospital with alcohol related diseases and injuries rose in 2005-2006 to 8,299, a jump of 40 per cent on figures three years ago.

A survey by charity Alcohol Concern found in 2005 that more than one in five 11-year-olds admitted to drinking. By the age of 12, drinkers start to outnumber non-drinkers.

Age limit

Frank Soodeen of Alcohol Concern said that the answer to cutting under-age drinking lay in using existing laws better rather than raising the age limit.

He said: 'If the current laws were better utilised that would go a long way to reducing alcohol related violence. For example a lot of people don't know that it is illegal to serve someone alcohol who is already very drunk.'

He said that a smart card to record the drinking of under-21s was, 'a very think tank idea' but added, 'there is definitely an argument for using technology to help people monitor their drinking.'

A Home Office spokesman said that there were no plans to raise the age limit to buy alcohol.

'The majority of people drink sensibly and responsibly and the government has no plans to raise the minimum drinking age. Instead, we are using a combination of effective education and tough enforcement to change the behaviour of the minority that don't.'

16 April 2007

© *The Press Association*

Responsible drinking tips

Enjoy your night out – without the hangover the next day

⇨ Drink water or soft drinks in between alcoholic drinks to dilute the alcohol.

⇨ Pace yourself. Slow down and take small sips not big gulps.

⇨ Eat something before or during drinking. Food makes the body absorb alcohol more slowly.

⇨ Change your drink. Make spirits into long drinks by topping up with more mixer, add soda water to white wine, or choose shandy rather than beer.

⇨ Watch out for larger measures at home or at a party compared with standard pub measures.

⇨ Know how to refuse a drink. You don't have to take one just because it's offered or take part in rounds you don't want. Similarly, don't pressure others into drinking.

⇨ Darker drinks like red wine, brandy and whisky give worse hangovers because of higher concentrations of chemicals called congeners.

⇨ Avoid top-ups so you can keep track of how much you are drinking.

⇨ Remember nights out don't have to be in the pub why not try the cinema, gym or theatre instead.

⇨ Learn the strengths of your drinks so you can stick to your own limits, bearing in mind the safe limits are 2/3 units per day for women and 3/4 units per day for men (but not every day).

⇨ The above information is reprinted with kind permission from Alcohol Focus Scotland. Visit www.alcohol-focus-scotland.org.uk for more information.

© *Alcohol Focus Scotland*

Wine lovers targeted to cut binge drinking

By Alex Berry and Nic Fleming

Middle-class wine lovers will be targeted alongside anti-social teenage binge drinkers as part of a new Government strategy being announced today to tackle the social and health impact of excessive drinking.

It is also expected to include plans to make people pay for damage they cause and treatment they need for injuries when drunk, as well as bigger fines for those selling drinks to under-age customers and better warnings about the dangers of alcohol.

A hard-hitting advertising campaign will also be launched, with the aim of making binge drinking as socially unacceptable as drink-driving.

It comes as doctors' leaders call for pubs and restaurants to display clear warnings about how many units of alcohol are contained in drinks they serve.

The British Medical Association yesterday said the information should be displayed on signs and posters in bars, and on wine lists.

Dr Vivienne Nathanson, the BMA's head of science and ethics, said the voluntary agreement between the Government and the drinks industry to include unit information on cans and bottles did not go far enough.

Today's Government strategy, being launched by Vernon Coaker, the Home Office minister, and Caroline Flint the health minister, is expected to widen the focus beyond teenagers and binge drinkers.

'We want to target the older drinkers, those that are maybe drinking one or two bottles of wine at home each evening. They do not realise the damage they are doing to their health and that they risk developing liver disease,' a Whitehall source said.

'There are growing numbers of people turning up in hospital with drink-related diseases and injuries. They are getting younger and more of them are turning up needing treatment.'

The Government strategy comes after Dr Nathanson called for further labelling and information measures in pubs and bars.

'People may think that one glass of wine equals one unit, but the new measures are two units and the big glasses are three units,' she said.

'If I go out and buy a bottle of wine or some cans of beer that's fine, but the trouble is when you're in a pub you don't ask to inspect the back of a bottle of wine, so we do need a form of labelling that goes up in pubs and restaurants.'

> Middle-class wine lovers will be targeted alongside anti-social teenage binge drinkers as part of a new Government strategy

'On the wine list it would say at the front whether wines were high, medium or low strength, and how many units in a bottle or different size glasses. There could be similar posters in pubs.'

'This is not about the nanny state, but the information state. The state's job is to give people information so that they can make informed choices.'

Mark Hastings, of the British Beer and Pub Association, said: 'The industry is already in discussion with the Government about how to improve people's understanding of units when they shop either in pubs or in supermarkets.'

He questioned whether posters were the right way to tackle the problem.

The BMA has also decided to back the Government's advice last week that pregnant women, and those trying for a baby, should drink no alcohol at all.

The previous recommendation was that one to two units of alcohol once or twice a week was acceptable.

The Government recommends that men do not regularly exceed three or four units a day and women do not exceed two or three units a day.

The Royal College of Obstetricians and Gynaecologists said it was sticking to its advice that moderate drinking was safe, leaving many potential mothers confused about who to believe.

5 June 2007

Alcohol health warnings

Europeans support alcohol health warnings to protect vulnerable, Eurobarometer reveals

Almost eight out of ten Europeans (77%) agree with putting warnings on alcohol bottles and adverts in order to warn pregnant women and drivers of the dangers of drinking alcohol, according to the results of the special Eurobarometer on Alcohol presented by the European Commission today. The survey reveals that European public opinion is, in general, sup-portive of measures aiming to protect vulnerable groups in society and to reduce alcohol-related road accidents. According to the data, men drink more than women, and one in ten Europeans usually drink five or more drinks in one session, which is the widely used definition of binge drinking. Binge drinking is a particular problem among young people, with 19% of the 15-24 age group usually binge drinking when consuming alcohol.

EU Health Commissioner Markos Kyprianou said: 'It is evident from this survey that EU citizens support measures crafted to protect specific groups in society, such as pregnant women, drivers and young people from the harmful effects of alcohol abuse and misuse. I am deeply concerned about the data showing that one in five young Europeans regularly binge drink.'

Protective measures

It is estimated that alcohol abuse and misuse kills 195,000 people a year in the EU. Harmful alcohol consumption is responsible for one in four deaths among young men aged 15-29. The vast majority of Europeans would welcome measures to protect vulnerable groups in society and to reduce deaths by road accidents. Only 21% disagree with putting health warnings on alcohol bottles and adverts in order to warn pregnant women and drivers of the dangers of consuming alcohol. 76% approve of banning alcohol advertising which targets young people.

Almost three quarters of Europeans (73%) surveyed would agree to the introduction of a lower blood alcohol level for young and novice drivers of 0.2 g/l, and 80% of respondents believe that random alcohol testing by police would reduce people's alcohol consumption before driving.

> One in ten Europeans usually drink five or more drinks in one session, which is the widely used definition of binge drinking for men

Men drink more, one in ten Europeans binge drink

More men than women drink alcohol and men also tend to consume more alcoholic beverages than women. According to the survey, 84% of male respondents said they had drunk alcohol in the past year. Among women, that percentage stood at 68%. Two thirds of Europeans said they had drunk alcohol in the past month. 35% of men admitted to having more than three drinks in one sitting and 79% of women noted they had less than two drinks on a day when they drink beer, wine or spirits.

One in ten Europeans usually drink five or more drinks in one session, which is the widely used definition of binge drinking for men. This is the same figure as in 2003 and is particularly high among the youngest respondents. Almost one in five young people in the 15-24 age group (19%) drink five or more alcoholic beverages in one session.

Among the population as a whole, there are considerable national variations, with 34% of Irish respondents saying they usually binge drink, and about one in four respondents from Finland (27%), the UK (24%) and Denmark (23%). On the other hand, only 2% of respondents in Italy and Greece and 4% in Portugal usually binge drink.

Price matters for young people

The survey indicates that higher prices would not reduce alcohol consumption for most people. 62% said they would not buy less alcoholic drinks if the price went up by 25%. One third (33%), though, claimed they would purchase less alcohol in case of such a price increase. However, younger respondents react more sensitively to alcohol price increases: 44% of the youngest respondents believe that they would buy less alcohol with a 25% price increase. Most Europeans (68%) believe that higher prices for alcohol would not discourage young people and heavy drinkers from consuming alcohol.

14 March 2007

⇨ The above information is reprinted with kind permission from the European Commission. Visit http://europa.eu for more information.

© *European Commission*

Government health warning for alcoholic drinks

New labels to include unit information

Alcoholic drinks will get new warning labels under a government scheme to be implemented by the end of 2008.

In a voluntary agreement between ministers and the industry, all drinks will be expected to carry details of units and recommended safe drinking levels on their labels.

At present, bottles and cans carry percentage details of alcohol and most carry unit information.

But the government now wants safety advice for pregnant women put on there as well as the recommendations for safe drinking and the drink's unit content.

One unit is equivalent to a small glass of wine, half a pint of beer or one pub measure of spirits.

The government recommends that men do not regularly exceed three or four units a day and women do not exceed two or three units a day.

Binge drinking

The move comes amid fears about the rise in binge drinking and an increase in alcohol-related diseases and death.

For beer, wines and spirits, unit information will be given per glass and per bottle.

The charity website – www.drinkaware.co.uk – will also be included on the labels.

Public health minister Caroline Flint said: 'This landmark, voluntary agreement will help people calculate, at a glance, how much they are drinking and whether they are staying within sensible drinking guidelines.

'We want to make it as simple as possible for people to keep an eye on how much they are drinking and help them take the responsibility for lessening the impact excess alcohol can have on their health.

'Although most spirits and beer labels for sale in the UK market and many supermarkets' own brands of beers, wines and spirits, do carry some information on unit content, people can miscalculate and lose track of how much they are drinking.

'Unit information combined with sensible drinking guidelines on the new labels will make it simpler for people to calculate how many units they are drinking and make easier for them to stick to the recommended limits.'

Better choices

A spokesman for the Portman group said its members, which represent more than 60 per cent of beer, wine and spirits manufacturers in the UK, already carry unit information.

Around 85 per cent of beer manufacturers already carry unit details on their labels.

Kevin Byrne, interim chief executive of Drinkaware, said: 'We welcome the new labelling on alcoholic drinks.

'We hope that by providing consumers with more readily accessible information, it will enable them to make better choices about how often and how much they drink.'

Government research shows that 86 per cent of people know units are a measure of alcohol and 69 per cent know the recommended limits.

However, only 13 per cent keep a check on the number of units they drink each week.

Three quarters (75 per cent) of people support the idea of labelling, Government surveys have shown.

The move will be supported with a new campaign next year to raise awareness of unit measurements.
29 May 2007

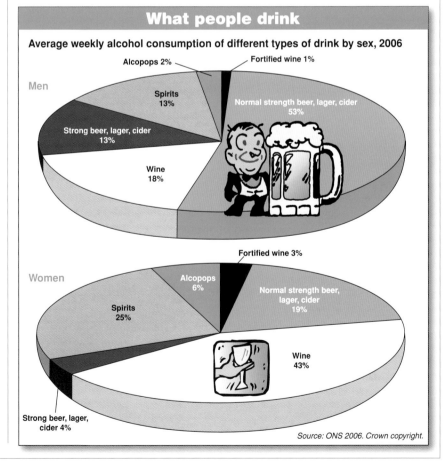

What people drink

Average weekly alcohol consumption of different types of drink by sex, 2006

Men
- Alcopops 2%
- Fortified wine 1%
- Spirits 13%
- Normal strength beer, lager, cider 53%
- Strong beer, lager, cider 13%
- Wine 18%

Women
- Fortified wine 3%
- Alcopops 6%
- Spirits 25%
- Normal strength beer, lager, cider 19%
- Wine 43%
- Strong beer, lager, cider 4%

Source: ONS 2006. Crown copyright.

Drinking during pregnancy

Pregnancy and alcohol – a dangerous cocktail says a new BMA report

Learning and physical disabilities and behavioural problems are part of fetal alcohol spectrum disorders [FASD]. These lifelong conditions can drastically impact on the lives of the individual and those around them. A new BMA report published today (Monday 4 June 2007) says the reality is that these conditions are completely preventable by not drinking any alcohol during pregnancy.

The report, 'Fetal alcohol spectrum disorders1', highlights how difficult it can be to detect FASD and how healthcare professionals need more guidance to help them diagnose and treat children suffering from the disorder.

The government in England has just revised its guidance and now advises pregnant women or women trying to conceive to avoid drinking alcohol. But if they do choose to drink, to minimise the risk to the baby, they should not consume more than one to two units of alcohol once or twice a week. However, the BMA report says this can be misinterpreted, as individuals may not clearly understand how many units correspond to what they are drinking. The alcoholic strengths of different beers and wines, and the considerable variation of standard measures used in bars and restaurants and in the home, can make it difficult for women to tell how many units they are consuming.

The new advice from the English government has been disputed by some medical experts and the BMA is now calling for clear, evidence-based guidelines on alcohol consumption during pregnancy and for women who are planning a pregnancy.

Dr Vivienne Nathanson, Head of BMA Science and Ethics, said today: 'The UK has one of the highest levels of binge-drinking in Europe and the highest rate of teenage pregnancies in Western Europe. Many women will not know they are pregnant during the early part of pregnancy, during which time they may continue to drink in their pre-pregnancy fashion with no awareness of the risk to their unborn child.'

There is proven risk that heavy drinking by pregnant women can cause these disorders in their children, says the BMA. The report states that evidence is continuing to emerge on the effects of low or moderate prenatal alcohol exposure and until there is clarification the only message is that it is not safe to drink any alcohol during pregnancy or when planning a pregnancy.

The government in England has just revised its guidance and now advises pregnant women or women trying to conceive to avoid drinking alcohol

---

Dr Nathanson, added: 'What is clear is that this is a complex concern and there is still so much that we do not know about this issue. It's important that women who drank alcohol before realising they were pregnant do not panic. But pregnant women should try to reduce their alcohol intake, or better still give up completely. If they are anxious they should talk to their doctor or midwife at their next antenatal appointment.

'We need to raise awareness of the emerging evidence on FASD among healthcare professionals. They need training and guidance on how to identify these disorders so that children are diagnosed quickly and get the help they need. Early intervention is crucial in decreasing the risk of additional problems commonly found in individuals affected by these disorders. These include mental health problems, disrupted school experience, alcohol and drug addictions. The lack of awareness and research in the UK on this subject, together with the complexity of the syndrome itself is leading to delays in diagnosis and referral.

'Healthcare professionals also need to get the message across to expectant mothers that consuming alcohol can cause irreversible harm to their unborn child. It's about giving people the right information so that they can act responsibly – and save children from completely preventable life-long disabilities.'

Recommendations in the report include:

- There is an urgent need for further UK and international research on FASD.
- Research should be undertaken to examine the relationship between different levels of pre-natal exposure and the range of conditions associated with FASD.
- The UK health departments should implement guidance and training programmes for healthcare professionals on the prevention, diagnosis and management of FASD.

The alcoholic strengths of different beers and wines, and the considerable variation of standard measures used in bars . . . can make it difficult for women to tell how many units they are consuming

---

- Women who are pregnant, or who are considering a pregnancy, should be advised not to consume any alcohol.
- Research should be undertaken to identify the most effective ways to educate the public about FASD and to alter drinking behaviour. This requires systematic studies that compare various universal strategies and their impacts across the different social groups.
- All healthcare professionals should provide clear and coherent advice for expectant mothers and anyone planning a pregnancy on the risks of maternal alcohol consumption. This should be provided by GPs as part of routine clinical care and targeted at women of childbearing age. Members of the antenatal care team should provide continued advice and support to expectant mothers throughout pregnancy.
- Any woman who is pregnant, or who is planning a pregnancy, and who has a suspected or confirmed history of alcohol consumption at low-to-moderate levels should be offered brief intervention counselling to help them stop drinking. This should occur at the earliest possible stage in a pregnancy and be considered as part of routine antenatal care where required.
- Any woman who is identified as being at high-risk of prenatal alcohol exposure should be offered referral to specialist alcohol services for appropriate treatment. Any referral should be followed up and assessed at regular intervals.

4 June 2007

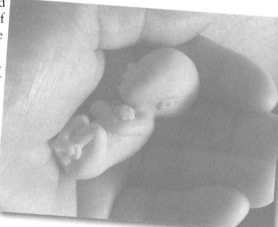

- The above information is re-printed with kind permission from the British Medical Association. Visit www.bma.org.uk for more information.

© BMA

Safe drinking confusion

The public are confused about drinking

A survey published in the British Medical Journal found that most shoppers don't know the recommended daily alcohol limit and many don't use alcohol labelling to help monitor their drinking. Heavy drinking can lead to heart disorders including high blood pressure and stroke.

Researchers Jan Gill and Fiona O'May, from Queen Mary University College in Scotland, asked 263 supermarket shoppers in Edinburgh about their knowledge of sensible drinking messages and awareness of alcohol labelling.

The Department of Health advises that men drink no more than 3-4 units of alcohol per day, and women should drink no more than 2-3 units. A 175ml glass of red or white wine contains around two units. A pint of ordinary strength lager also has two units.

The survey found that most of those questioned were able to define roughly what a unit of alcohol was – only 14 per cent of women and 16 per cent of men were unable to give a response.

But knowledge of the recommended daily guidance was poor. Only 8 per cent knew that women were limited to 2-3 units and 5 per cent knew that men were limited to 3-4 units a day. Only 25 per cent of women and 19 per cent of men said they used the unit system to monitor their own personal drinking.

Of the 46 per cent of people who said they preferred drinking wine, 22 per cent could give no estimate of the number of units in a bottle and 36 per cent thought it was seven or fewer units – the right answer is about nine.

The researchers said: 'This pilot study highlights considerable confusion about sensible drinking messages in the UK. Few respondents used the unit system to monitor their drinking.'

They said that current educational initiatives in the UK may fail to help adults wishing to drink sensibly due to confusion over the guidelines.

- The above information is reprinted with kind permission from Which?. Visit www.which.co.uk for more information.

© Which? 2007

Overcoming a drink problem

If you think you drink too much, then chances are you do. Nobody can force you to reduce your alcohol intake, or make you seek professional help. The only person who can take responsibility for that is you. If you've woken up to the fact that you need to cut down or quit, here are some tips to help

Review your lifestyle

Identify those times and places when you're most likely to reach for a drink. From the bar after work to the weekend with friends, if you know you'll be tempted then think about steering clear. Alternatively, try turning up later than usual, to minimise your drinking time, or kick off with a soft drink to stop you from feeling so thirsty.

Drink for the right reasons

Try to associate drinking with celebrations, cultural and religious events, rather than a means of blotting out your problems or propping up your self-confidence. Also think of alcohol as something you do as a complement to another activity, instead of something you turn to for its own sake.

Pace yourself

Binge drinking is dangerous, as your body can only process one unit of alcohol per hour. The more rapidly you drink the more intense the effects will be, but that doesn't make the experience any more enjoyable. If you find it hard to apply the booze brakes, try putting your drink down more often. If it isn't in your hand all the time, you're less likely to drink it so quickly.

Learn new bar tricks

If you're at the bar with a glass in your hand, try talking more. Use your mouth for something other than boozing and you're less likely to fall down at the end of the evening. Getting in something to eat can also have the same stalling effect, though be careful with salty snacks, as it could just stoke your thirst.

Know your limit

Before you start drinking, be sure you know when to stop. This can be hard when everyone else is boozing, but practice makes perfect. It also avoids bad hangovers.

Take a break from boozing

If you're worried about drinking, but you don't fancy quitting completely, then set aside an alcohol-free period every now and then. It might be one day in a week or a month, but even a temporary hop onto the wagon can be enough to keep the issue alive in your mind. Ultimately, the more switched on you can be about your alcohol intake the less likely it is that you'll run into problems.

Seeking help

Facing up to the fact that you may have a drink problem takes guts. It is perhaps the most courageous step you can take towards regaining control over your life. Help is out there too, from confidential telephone support to face-to-face counselling and more, but it's down to you to ask.

⇨ The above information is reprinted with kind permission from TheSite.org. Visit www.thesite.org for more information.

© TheSite.org

Alcohol misuse

Recommendations

If you answer 'yes' to two or more of the following questions, you need to think about your alcohol intake:

⇨ Have you ever thought you should cut down on your drinking?
⇨ Have other people ever annoyed you by commenting on your drinking?
⇨ Do you ever feel guilty about the amount of alcohol you are drinking?
⇨ Have you ever taken a drink in the morning to relieve the symptoms of alcohol (commonly known as hair of the dog or an eye-opener)?

If you answer 'yes' to three or more of the following questions, you should consider seeking help from your GP who will be able to refer you to a specialist:

⇨ If you are a man, are you drinking more than 50 units of alcohol a week?
⇨ If you are a woman, are you drinking more than 35 units a week?
⇨ Do you have a strong desire or need to drink alcohol?
⇨ Do you find it difficult to resist the urge to drink, stop drinking, or to control the amount that you drink?
⇨ Does your behaviour change, or do you feel differently, if you cannot get a drink?
⇨ Do you drink to relieve or prevent those feelings?
⇨ Do you seem to be able to drink more than most other people around you? Do you have a higher tolerance to alcohol than others?
⇨ Does the desire to drink, or the effects of alcohol, stop you taking part in your other interests and pleasures?
⇨ Do you still drink, despite knowing about the harmful consequences?

⇨ The above information is reprinted with kind permission from NHS Direct. Visit www.nhsdirect.nhs.uk for more information.

© NHS Direct

The bigger picture

Alcohol services

Figures in August 2006 show that while 3.5 million people used drugs in the last year, 8.2 million people have an alcohol disorder. Meanwhile, the government Information Centre for Health and Social Care revealed that alcohol-related illness has reached record levels. In-patient care for people with mental health or behavioural disorders resulting from alcohol misuse increased by 75 per cent from 1995 to 2005, and from 72,500 admissions to 126,300, it said. Numbers admitted to hospital with liver disease due to alcohol have more than doubled over the past 10 years.

No wonder then, that in January 2005 the government published its Drinking Responsibly consultation document aimed at curbing under-age and binge drinking. And an independent charitable trust aimed at changing the UK's drinking culture is expected to be up and running in the next few months. The Drinkaware Trust will be voluntarily funded by the alcohol industry. It will bring together industry, charities, lobby groups, medical experts and professionals in the field to address alcohol misuse across the UK.

Licensing laws

Historically, though, tackling alcohol problems has always taken a back seat compared with the war on drugs being waged by the government. And there are fears that any progress could be scuppered by the new licensing laws introduced in England and Wales in November 2005 which offer the potential for pubs and clubs to stay open 24 hours a day, seven days a week. Greater availability of alcohol encourages increased consumption and those in the alcohol treatment sector fear it will lead to more people needing specialist support.

As it is, an average of just one in 18 problem drinkers in England can access the treatment services they need, according to Department of Health figures in February 2006. In the north east the proportion falls to less than one in 100. This prompted the charity Alcohol Concern to bemoan the 'shocking lack of services'.

Perhaps this is why, in September 2006, ministers announced that information about drug and alcohol abusers will be shared by the police, health and social services under new proposals to fight crime and help those most at risk.

Figures in August 2006 show that while 3.5 million people used drugs in the last year, 8.2 million people have an alcohol disorder

---

The government first pledged to combat alcohol misuse in its white paper 'Saving Lives: Our Healthier Nation' in July 1999, following this with an undertaking in the NHS Plan that the Department of Health would implement a strategy for England by 2004.

But England was still bringing up the rear: in May 2000, the Tackling Substance Misuse in Wales strategy was produced; Northern Ireland published its Strategy for Reducing Alcohol Related Harm in September 2000; and Scotland announced its Plan for Action on Alcohol Problems in January 2002.

Back in England, a Cabinet Office strategy unit was established in 2002 to review and analyse policy in England. In October 2002, the unit published a consultation document with the Department of Health called The National Alcohol Harm Reduction Strategy. Consultation ended in January 2003.

The strategy unit's interim analysis estimated that alcohol misuse was costing about £20 billion a year. This is made up of alcohol-related health disorders and disease, crime and anti-social behaviour, loss of productivity in the workplace, and problems for those who misuse alcohol and their families, including domestic violence.

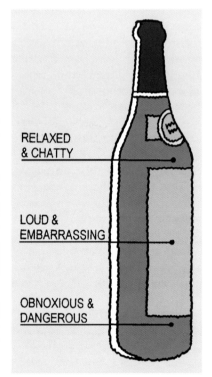

RELAXED & CHATTY

LOUD & EMBARRASSING

OBNOXIOUS & DANGEROUS

It said that the annual cost includes:
⇨ 1.2 million violent incidents.
⇨ 360,000 incidents of domestic violence are linked to alcohol.
⇨ Increased anti-social behaviour and fear of crime.
⇨ £95 million on specialist alcohol treatment.
⇨ Over 30,000 hospital admissions for alcohol dependence syndrome.
⇨ Up to 22,000 premature deaths annually.
⇨ At peak times, up to 70 per cent of all admissions to A&E departments.
⇨ Up to 1,000 suicides.
⇨ Up to 17 million working days lost.
⇨ Between 780,000 and 1.3 million children affected by parental alcohol problems.
⇨ Increased divorce.

The alcohol harm reduction strategy

But, after much anticipation, the alcohol harm reduction strategy was unveiled in March 2004. It set out a cross-government approach that relies on creating a partnership at national and local levels between government, the drinks industry, health and police services, and individuals and communities to tackle alcohol misuse.

It has four key aims:

⇨ To improve the information available to individuals and start a process of change in the culture of drinking to get drunk: for example, providing alcohol education in schools; reviewing the code of practice for TV advertising to ensure that it does not target young drinkers or glamorise irresponsible behaviour.

⇨ To better identify and treat alcohol misuse: for example, piloting schemes to see if earlier identification and treatment can improve health and also have longer-term savings; better help for vulnerable people, including homeless people, drug addicts, people with mental health problems and young people.

⇨ To prevent and tackle alcohol-related crime and disorder and deliver improved services to victims and witnesses: for example, greater use of the new fixed penalty fines for anti-social behaviour.

⇨ To work with the industry in tackling the harms caused by alcohol: for example, at national level there will be a social responsibility charter for drinks producers and at local level, a new code of good conduct scheme for retailers, pubs and clubs, led by the local authority. Initially, participation in these schemes will be voluntary.

Progress on the strategy will be measured regularly against indicators and the government will take stock of how things are going in 2007.

All these measures show that alcohol is now on the agenda. However, whether the government puts as much money into tackling alcohol misuse as it has into drug misuse is unlikely. For example, in December 2002, it announced it would be investing £1.5 billion to tackle drug misuse.

However, while the new alcohol strategy mentions funding for pilot schemes to find out whether earlier identification and treatment of those with alcohol problems can improve health and lead to longer-term savings – a move that many in the field feel is a waste of money anyway as the answer is obvious – it makes no mention of how much money the government is prepared to put into treatment services. And without the back-up of funding, the new strategy will make little difference.

Facts and figures

Researchers believe the first experiences of drinking begin at about 11-years-old, but can be as early as eight. About 1,000 under-15s are admitted to hospital every year with alcohol poisoning. One in 13 people are dependent on alcohol, that's twice the number dependent on drugs. According to the British Crime Survey 2000, alcohol misuse is implicated in 40 per cent of violent crimes.

In 2001, a survey by the European School Survey Project on Alcohol and Other Drugs (Espad) found that 15 to 16-year-olds in the UK drink more than their European counterparts. The Alcohol and Health Research Centre conducted the UK part of the survey. It found that 91 per cent of respondents had been drinking alcohol during the past 12 months. Over two-thirds of UK pupils had been drunk in the previous year, compared with a European average of 52 per cent.

And more recent figures show that alcohol-related deaths among young women have tripled in 20 years and an average of two young men and one young woman now die every day in England and Wales from the effects of alcohol. And the trend of people dying younger from alcohol-related causes is predicted to continue.

An estimated 920,000 children live in families where one or both parents have problems with alcohol. In August 2006, academics and 11 charities including Turning Point and Alcohol Concern, wrote to children's minister Beverley Hughes calling for urgent action to tackle the misery of 1.3 million children affected by parental alcohol abuse. They called on the government to launch a national inquiry into the impact of parental alcohol abuse and to develop new services for children and parents.

Research has also shown that heavy drinking can contribute to anxiety and depression, and accelerate or uncover a predisposition to a psychiatric disorder or psychosis.
6 February 2007

⇨ The above information is reprinted with kind permission from Community Care. Visit www.communitycare.co.uk for more information.

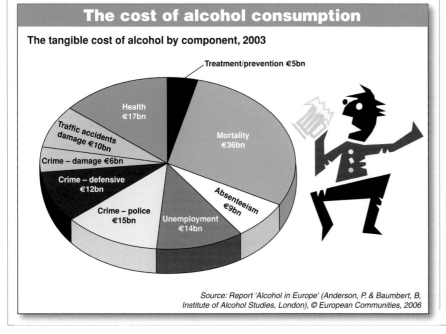

The cost of alcohol consumption

The tangible cost of alcohol by component, 2003

- Treatment/prevention €5bn
- Health €17bn
- Traffic accidents damage €10bn
- Crime – damage €6bn
- Crime – defensive €12bn
- Crime – police €15bn
- Unemployment €14bn
- Absenteeism €9bn
- Mortality €36bn

Source: Report 'Alcohol in Europe' (Anderson, P. & Baumbert, B, Institute of Alcohol Studies, London), © European Communities, 2006

Alcohol misuse – treatment

Information from NHS Direct

As with any addiction, if you are an alcoholic, the first step is to acknowledge that you have a problem. Once you have accepted that you have a problem, the next step is to seek help.

If you have an alcohol problem, there are many different professional services and support groups that can help you to reduce your alcohol consumption, and give you the advice and support that you need to stop drinking altogether.

It is estimated that about 1 in 3 people who have an alcohol problem are able to reduce their drinking, or stop drinking altogether, without the need for professional help

---

Group therapy sessions, or one-to-one counselling with trained medical and psychiatric professionals, are two common methods that may be recommended if you have an alcohol related problem. As well as attending therapy sessions, you may also receive specific treatment for any associated nutritional problems, or other secondary effects, that you may have.

Self help
It is estimated that about 1 in 3 people who have an alcohol problem are able to reduce their drinking, or stop drinking altogether, without the need for professional help. There are many self help books, leaflets, and web sites available that offer help and advice about how you can stop or reduce drinking.

Counselling
Some people who have a drinking problem find it extremely useful to talk about their situation with their GP or practice nurse. You may then be referred to a specially trained counsellor who will discuss, in more detail, the issues surrounding your drinking problem, and help you to plan how you can control and manage your drinking. Sometimes, cognitive-behaviour therapy (CBT) is used to treat alcoholism. This therapy is designed to help you change your attitude and behaviour towards alcohol.

Treating other conditions
Sometimes, drinking alcohol is used to mask a range of other, underlying health problems. For example, people with an alcohol related problem often also have problems with stress, anxiety, depression, or other mental health problems. If you feel you may have a mental health problem, you should see your GP who will be able to prescribe medication or recommend other forms of treatment for you.

Always remember that heavy drinking is not the answer and, in the long-term, it is likely to make any underlying condition that you have, worse.

Detoxification
Detoxification or detox is a process that involves taking a short course of medication in order to prevent you having withdrawal symptoms when you stop drinking alcohol. Benzodiazepine medicines, such as chlordiazepoxide, are often used for detox. Usually, a high dose of medication will be prescribed for the first day that you stop drinking alcohol, before being gradually reduced over the next 5-7 days. This should reduce any unpleasant withdrawal symptoms that you might otherwise have. You should not drink any alcohol during the period of detoxification.

Staying off alcohol
Sometimes, people who successfully go through the detox process, start drinking again at some point, and it may take several attempts before you manage to significantly reduce your alcohol consumption, or are able to stop altogether.

However, you are more likely to be successful, if you have counselling, or other support from your family, friends, your GP, local alcohol support groups, and other self help groups.

Last updated on 18 May 2007

⇨ The above information is reprinted with kind permission from NHS Direct. Visit www.nhsdirect.nhs.uk for more information.

Battling the booze

New training technique helps alcoholics in battle with the booze

A new training technique developed in the UK is proving successful in helping excessive drinkers curb their alcohol abuse. Researchers funded by the Economic and Social Research Council have experimentally tested a computer-based training programme which helps abusive drinkers pay less attention to alcohol, feel more in control of their drinking and drink less.

Researchers at the University of Wales found that excessive drinkers cut down significantly on their drinking following their participation in this project's newly developed Alcohol Attention-Control Training Programme (AACTP). Moreover, excessive drinkers were found to have maintained this improvement at a three-month follow-up assessment.

'AACTP is now a tried and tested training programme which can help improve the effectiveness of treatment for alcohol-related problems,' explains researcher Professor W. Miles Cox. 'AACTP is also a highly accessible tool in that it will eventually offer excessive drinkers the opportunity to participate in this training in their own home over the Internet.'

AACTP works by helping excessive drinkers become less distracted by the alcohol stimuli they see around them – stimuli which range from pictures of alcoholic beverages to bottles of alcohol in the local off-licence window or on the shelves of a supermarket.

'Excessive drinkers unconsciously pay too much attention to the alcohol-related stimuli that surround us all,' Professor Cox points out. 'When excessive drinkers encounter drink-related stimuli, this activates automatic thought processes which stimulate them to want a drink and to actually take a drink. Hence the simple consequence of helping excessive drinkers pay less attention to alcohol in their environment is that they gain more confidence in their ability to control their own behaviour, and then they drink less.'

The ACCTP training procedure developed by Professor W. Miles Cox and Dr Javad S. Fadardi is a computerised programme based on goal-setting techniques with immediate feedback. For example, two bottles – an alcoholic and non-alcoholic one – appear on the computer screen each surrounded by a different colour. The participant must then identify the colour surrounding the non-alcoholic bottle as quickly as possible.

'This training causes people to become faster at ignoring alcoholic stimuli,' explains Professor Cox. 'Over a course of four sessions, our sample of excessive drinkers showed significant reductions in their attentional focus on alcohol which translated into lower alcohol consumption.'

In terms of conquering alcohol addiction, Professor Cox argues that 'different interventions are required by different people. It could be that AACTP is all that is required to halt alcohol abuse in an early stage drinker. But others may need further help to curb their drinking habit. While ACCTP can reduce a person's bias towards alcohol, the reality for many is that when they stop drinking it creates a void in their lives. Permanent change in drinking habits usually requires a person to restructure their lives in ways that can fill that void.'
22 July 2006

⇨ Information from the Economic and Social Research Council. Visit www.esrcsocietytoday.ac.uk for more information.

© ESRC

AA meetings

The two most common kinds of AA meetings

Open meetings

As the term suggests, meetings of this type are open to alcoholics and their families and to anyone interested in solving a personal drinking problem or helping someone else to solve such a problem.

Most open meetings follow a more or less set pattern, although distinctive variations have developed in some areas. A chairperson describes the A.A. program briefly for the benefit of newcomers in the audience and introduces one, two or three speakers who relate their personal drinking histories and may give their personal interpretation of A.A.

Midway through the meeting there is usually a period for local A.A. announcements, and a treasurer passes the hat to defray costs of the meeting hall, literature, and incidental expenses. The meeting adjourns, often followed by informal visiting over coffee or other light refreshments.

Closed meetings

These meetings are limited to alcoholics. They provide an opportunity for members to share with one another on problems related to drinking patterns and attempts to achieve stable sobriety. They also permit detailed discussion of various elements in the recovery program.

Guests at A.A. open meetings are reminded that any opinions or interpretations they may hear are solely those of the speaker involved. All members are free to interpret the recovery program in their own terms, but none can speak for the local group or for A.A. as a whole.

⇨ The above information is reprinted with kind permission from the General Service Board of Alcoholics Anonymous (Great Britain) Limited. Visit www.alcoholics-anonymous.org.uk for more information.
© General Service Board of Alcoholics Anonymous (Great Britain) Limited

⇨ Most wines are produced with an ABV of around 10-13% in a standard 750ml bottle containing 7-10 units of alcohol. Wines from hotter climates such as Italian and Californian wines tend to be stronger at 12 to 13% ABV while those from cooler climates such as Germany are usually 8 to 10%. (page 1)

⇨ The manufacture, sale, distribution and purchase of alcohol is mainly controlled by the 1964 Licensing Act. (page 2)

⇨ There are different licences governing the sale of alcohol. Full 'on licenses' are granted to pubs and clubs and mean alcohol can be drunk on the premises. 'Off licenses' are granted to off- licenses, shops and supermarkets where alcohol cannot be consumed on the premises. 'Restaurant licenses' permit the sale of alcohol and consumption on the premises if accompanied by a meal. Licensing laws also restrict the times at which alcohol can be sold and consumed. (page 2)

⇨ Alcohol is absorbed into the blood-stream and starts to have an effect within 5 to 10 minutes. The effect can last for several hours, depending on the amount consumed. (page 3)

⇨ Teenagers who drink alcohol with their parents are less likely to binge drink, according to a survey of 10,000 children which backs the continental style of introducing teenagers to small amounts of alcohol early. (page 5)

⇨ Globally, alcohol consumption has increased in recent decades, with all or most of that increase in developing countries. (page 6)

⇨ Alcohol is estimated to cause about 20-30% worldwide of oesophageal cancer, liver cancer, cirrhosis of the liver, homicide, epilepsy, and motor vehicle accidents. (page 6)

⇨ The belief that one glass of wine equals one unit is only true when that glass contains 125ml and the wine is around 8 per cent ABV (alcohol by volume). Today, many wines are 12 or 13 per cent ABV, and most standard wine glasses contain 175ml – 2.3 units – and larger wine glasses contain 250ml, which is equal to 3 units. (page 10)

⇨ Fifty eight per cent of those who had drunk beer in the last year knew that a unit of beer is half a pint but one in five (20 per cent) gave an amount that was wrong. (page 11)

⇨ 18.2% of adults binge drink more than double the daily recommended limit at least once a week. (page 13)

⇨ UK teenagers report some of the highest levels of life-time drunkenness – 27% report having been drunk 20 times or more in their life time. In addition 36% report being drunk at age of 13 years. (page 15)

⇨ Young people are thought to be particularly susceptible to drinks advertising. Studies show that the more appreciative they are of advertising, the more likely they are to drink now and in the future. (page 17)

⇨ The amount of alcohol consumed by girls aged between 11-13 has increased by 82.6% between 2000-2006, while for boys the number has gone up by 43.4% during the same period. (page 20)

⇨ 62% of people surveyed by YouGov felt that tobacco and alcohol, even if they remain legal, should be classified according to how much harm they can cause in the same way as illegal drugs. (page 22)

⇨ Serious violence-related injuries fell by 2% in England and Wales last year, despite the change in pub opening hours, according to a new Cardiff University study. (page 23)

⇨ According to a survey of 1,000 drivers by Brake, the road safety charity, half of drivers admit to drink-driving (after drinking any amount of alcohol at least once in the last twelve months), and one in four drivers admit to driving after drinking an amount of alcohol they know is affecting their driving. (page 24)

⇨ Most men are OK drinking 3 to 4 units a day, most women for 2 to 3. But if men consistently drink 4 or more units a day, the health risks start to accumulate. The same goes for women who consistently drink 3 or more units a day. (page 26)

⇨ A woman drinking the same amount as a man of exactly the same size will get intoxicated faster because she has a lower proportion of water in her body weight. (page 27)

⇨ Almost eight out of ten Europeans (77%) agree with putting warnings on alcohol bottles and adverts in order to warn pregnant women and drivers of the dangers of drinking alcohol. (page 31)

⇨ A survey published in the British Medical Journal found that most shoppers don't know the recommended daily alcohol limit and many don't use alcohol labelling to help monitor their drinking. (page 34)

ABV
This stands for alcohol by volume, and indicates what percentage of the total liquid is actually alcohol. It is always given on drinks labels in the UK.

Alcohol
The type of alcohol used in beverages is called ethanol, or ethyl alcohol. It is a chemical compound created during the fermentation process, and when taken internally can produce intoxication. Alcohol content is expressed as a percentage of volume or weight. Beer, lager and cider are usually about one part ethanol to 20 parts water although some brands may be twice as strong as others. Wine is about twice to four times as strong and distilled spirits such as whisky, rum and gin are about half water and half ethanol.

Alcoholism
Alcohol is a drug, and an addictive substance. Someone can become dependent on alcohol: that person can be referred to as an alcoholic, and their addition is called alcoholism. It is often difficult for an alcoholic to overcome their addiction without help of some kind, often from a support group such as Alcoholics Anonymous. Groups like this will usually advocate complete abstinence from alcohol for recovering alcoholics.

Alcopops
An alcopop is a name applied to an alcoholic drink which has been flavoured to taste like a soft drink, often disguising the taste of the alcohol to some extent. Most have an ABV of 4-5.5%. Some critics have blamed this type of drink for a rise in underage drinking, claiming drinks flavoured like cola or lemonade are more appealing to young people.

Binge drinking
Drinking to excess/intoxication. The commonly accepted definition of binge drinking is the intake of five or more drinks at any one time for a man, and four or more for a woman. There is evidence that binge drinking in the UK is rising, especially among young people, with the proportion of 15-16 year olds drinking at this level one of the highest in Europe.

Depressant
A depressant is a type of drug which causes sedation and drowsiness. Alcohol is a depressant, although many mistakenly believe it to be a stimulant.

Drink driving
Being in charge of a motor vehicle while intoxicated – this is a criminal offence. The current drink-drive limit in the UK is 80mg of alcohol per 100ml of blood, significantly higher than the majority of EU countries (the EC recommends a limit of 50mg of alcohol per 100ml of blood or less). Road safety charity Brake and other groups recommend drinking no alcohol at all before driving. Drink-drive deaths account for one in six road deaths, and 11 people are killed by drunk drivers on UK roads every week.

Drunkenness
This is the most common way of describing the state of being intoxicated due to alcohol. Many different slang words are also used, including pissed, trolleyed, hammered, muntered, bladdered, trashed and many others. Behaviour while under the influence of alcohol will depend on the amount drunk and the strength of the alcohol consumed, as well as a number of other factors including age, sex, weight, tiredness and whether food has been consumed. Those in the early stages of drunkenness may feel relaxed and less inhibited. As more alcohol is drunk, drinkers may experience a variety of effects, including a lack of coordination, slurred speech and aggressiveness. Heavy intake may result in alcohol poisoning.

Hangover
'Hangover' is the term used to describe the various symptoms which follow excessive alcohol intake. A hangover will most commonly involve some or all of the following: headache, nausea, fatigue, dehydration, a sensitivity to light and noise. Contrary to popular belief, the only true cure for a hangover is time and plenty of fluids, in order to give the system a chance to rehydrate.

Licensing hours
'Licensing' refers to the licence required for places such as pubs, restaurants and hotels to legally sell alcohol for consumption on the premises. By law, sale of alcohol can only take place at certain times – the 'licensing hours'. A change in the law in November 2005 altered the licensing regulations so that licensed premises can now apply to serve alcohol for a longer time each day (previously, sale of alcohol on licensed premises was restricted to 11pm on weeknights, and 10.30pm on Sundays). This is sometimes referred to as the '24-hour drinking' law.

Unit
A measure of alcohol used to determine medical guidelines as to what are supposed to be safe levels of drinking for men and women per week. Safe drinking limits are given as daily maximums – three to four units a day for men and two to three a day for women. One pint of normal strength lager usually contains about two units of alcohol, as does a 175ml glass of 12% wine. A unit is 8 grams of pure alcohol. Units are calculated by multiplying the amount of alcohol in millilitres by its ABV, and dividing by one thousand.

INDEX

Additional Resources

Other Issues titles

If you are interested in researching further some of the issues raised in *Problem Drinking*, you may like to read the following titles in the **Issues** series:

⇨ Vol. 114 Drug Abuse (ISBN 978 1 86168 347 2)

⇨ Vol. 128 The Cannabis Issue (ISBN 978 1 86168 374 8)

⇨ Vol. 128 Smoking Trends (ISBN 978 1 86168 411 0)

For more information about these titles, visit our website at www.independence.co.uk/publicationslist

Useful organisations

You may find the websites of the following organisations useful for further research:

⇨ National Association for Children of Alcoholics: www.nacoa.org.uk

⇨ Alcoholics Anonymous: www.alcoholics-anonymous.org.uk

⇨ Alcohol Focus Scotland: www.alcohol-focus-scotland.org.uk

⇨ Alcohol Concern: www.alcoholconcern.org.uk

ACKNOWLEDGEMENTS

The publisher is grateful for permission to reproduce the following material.

While every care has been taken to trace and acknowledge copyright, the publisher tenders its apology for any accidental infringement or where copyright has proved untraceable. The publisher would be pleased to come to a suitable arrangement in any such case with the rightful owner.

Chapter One: Alcohol Trends

Alcohol, © DrugScope, *Alcohol myths and facts*, © Alcohol Focus Scotland, *Cutting teen drinking*, © Guardian Newspapers Ltd, *Alcohol use internationally*, © World Health Organization, *Factors affecting drink*, © TheSite.org, *Clever girls are more likely to binge-drink*, © Associated Newspapers Ltd, *Drinking*, © Crown copyright is reproduced with the permission of Her Majesty's Stationery Office, *The mid-life bingers*, © Associated Newspapers Ltd, *Drinking: adults' behaviour and knowledge in 2006*, © Crown copyright is reproduced with the permission of Her Majesty's Stationery Office, *Binge drinking addicts*, © Guardian Newspapers Ltd, *Binge drinking*, © TheSite.org, *Young people's drinking*, © Alcohol Concern, *Does TV encourage teenage drinking?*, © Institute of Alcohol Studies, *Children and alcohol*, Alcohol Concern, *Alcohol and adolescence*, © Alcoweb, *How dangerous is alcohol?*, © Guardian Newspapers Ltd, *Crime and licensing hours*, © Cardiff University, *Drink-driving*, © Brake.

Chapter Two: Facing Alcohol Abuse

Frequently asked questions about alcohol, © Addiction Recovery Agency, *Questions and answers on responsible drinking*, © Portman Group, *Tackling underage drinking*, © Crown copyright is reproduced with the permission of Her Majesty's Stationery Office, *Raise drinking age to 21, says think tank*, © The Press Association, *Responsible drinking tips*, © Alcohol Focus Scotland, *Wine lovers targeted to cut binge drinking*, © Telegraph Group Ltd, *Alcohol health warnings*, © European Commission, *Government health warning for alcoholic drinks*, © The Press Association, *Drinking during pregnancy*, © British Medical Association, *Safe drinking confusion*, © Which? 2007, *Overcoming a drink problem*, © TheSite.org, *Alcohol misuse*, © NHS Direct, *The bigger picture*, © Community Care, *Alcohol misuse – treatment*, © NHS Direct, *Battling the booze*, © Economic and Social Research Council, *AA meetings*, © General Service Board of Alcoholics Anonymous (Great Britain) Ltd.

Illustrations

Pages 1, 14, 26, 31: Simon Kneebone; pages 8, 19: Bev Aisbett; pages 9, 20, 30, 36: Don Hatcher; pages 13, 22, 33, 38: Angelo Madrid.

Photographs

Page 2: Eyup Salman; page 21: Patti Adair; page 24: Armin Hanisch; page 34: Bill Davenport

And with thanks to the team: Mary Chapman, Sophie Crewdson, Sandra Dennis and Jan Haskell.

Lisa Firth and Cobi Smith
Cambridge
September, 2007